For Joan

Published by Hampshire County Recreation, North Hill Close, Andover Road, Winchester, Hampshire.

Typeset by Tigertype of Alresford, 26 The Dean, Alresford, Hants.

Designed by Orchard Studios Ltd., Whaddon Lane, Owslebury, Winchester, Hampshire.

Printed by Borcombe Printers Ltd, Unit 6, Budds Lane, Romsey, Hampshire.

ISBN 0 948 176 03 2

Walks in Wessex

THE TEST WAY

& THE CLARENDON WAY

BARRY SHURLOCK

HAMPSHIRE COUNTY COUNCIL
Recreation Department
Winchester

Acknowledgements

Most of the background material used in this guide came from the published sources listed under Further Reading on p. 126. I am most grateful to Philippa Stevens, Local Studies Librarian at the Winchester District Library, for helpful advice on the extensive collection of books on Hampshire which she administers.

David Johnston of the Department of Extra-Mural Studies, Southampton University, kindly gave me advice on Roman history, while Elizabeth Evans and Elspeth Hampson made available material on their respective localities of King's Somborne and Broughton. My friend Albert Cooper, through his local researches on the Liberal politician Lord Eversley, has highlighted the contributions to the cause of commoners' rights made by that man while he lived a stone's throw from my present home.

John Holder of the County Recreation Department has, for the second time, been my editor and has undertaken with great care the painful process of cutting the text to size.

Barry Shurlock
Abbot's Worthy, Hampshire

INTRODUCTION

'If Hampshire is attractive on the seaboard, inland she is a delight, varied in charm, soft, smiling, and winning everywhere.'

Telford Varley, 1909

This book is a detailed guide to the routes of two long-distance footpaths which span the breadth of Hampshire like a huge cross. The Test Way runs between Totton, near Southampton, in the south and Inkpen Beacon, near Combe, in the north, while the Clarendon Way links the two cathedral cities of Salisbury and Winchester.

Since the two paths intersect — near King's Somborne — this book is in fact a guide to six possible long-distance routes, each of which can of course be walked in either direction.

Winchester, Salisbury and Totton can be reached relatively easily by public transport or other means, though Combe, perched as it is on a remote scarp of the downs, presents problems of access that require individual solutions.

The Test Way, which has been signposted since 1984, follows the course of Hampshire's finest chalk stream, from its tidal waters at Totton to the clear, sparkling waters of its upper reaches at Longparish. Here the path leaves the main river and pursues the even-clearer waters of its tributary, the Bourne Rivulet, into the high lands of north-west Hampshire and the borders of Berkshire and Wiltshire.

Overall the Test Way covers a distance of 50 miles — a journey through some of the finest countryside in Southern England. People from all over the world come to the Test, not only for its renowned trout fishing but also for the charms of its meadows and villages. The Test Way provides a leisurely way to soak up the balmy atmosphere of this terrain, to explore its churches and village centres, to observe its birds and river life, or amble through open country which is as unhurried as ever.

From Totton the Test Way proceeds to the small town of Romsey, famous for its great abbey church, and then on to Stockbridge, a former market town which is still well tuned to the needs of country life. The path then passes through the heart of the Test country, through villages which have been preserved and fostered because they are dear to their inhabitants.

Beyond Longparish the character of the walk changes. The gentle reaches of the Test give way gradually to the steep slopes of the Hampshire Highlands and the brisker waters of the Bourne. No part of any English county can, of course, be called 'unknown' any more, but this section of the footpath passes through country which as 'unknown' as anywhere in the South.

The Test Way climbs to a dramatic ending: the walker is left at the top of a steep north-facing chalk scarp, looking across the western edge of the London Basin towards the heartlands of England. To the east and west stretch high lands that water the Southern Counties via small valleys that have charm, but never rival that of the Test. The other long-distance footpath described in this book, the newly-marked Clarendon Way, cuts across some of these valleys, keeping elsewhere to old ridgeways that must have been walked for centuries, even millennia.

The Clarendon Way takes its name from the former medieval palace which it passes on the outskirts of Salisbury. One of the delights of the walk is that it starts and ends in a fine cathedral city. Even a fleeting interest in the past must surely be awakened by the squat mass of Winchester Cathedral or the towering spire and delicate vaulting of its Wiltshire cousin!

Salisbury is a medieval 'new town', a county town and market centre with a large variety of shopping facilities. Still dominated by the presence of its cathedral, it is nonetheless a place with many other attractions, including a repertory theatre that draws its clientele from a wide area.

The Clarendon Way climbs out of the city along the route of an old Saxon road, past the site of Clarendon Palace and through deep woods to the former forest village of Pitton. All along the route to Winchester are reminders that this area of Hampshire, like many others, was heavily wooded and provided sport, recreation and food for kings and their court.

The path continues via Winterslow, once the home of William Hazlitt, and then follows the route of the former Roman road which ran between Old Sarum, just outside modern Salisbury, and Winchester. The rest of the Clarendon Way flits on and off the old Roman route, via the charming villages of Broughton and King's Somborne. There are long stretches of open downland with challenging gradients and fine views, culminating in Farley Mount Country Park on the outskirts of Winchester.

The footpath comes off the high ground via an old road which gives the walker a panoramic view of the old cathedral city, which by itself offers enjoyment for a day or more. Winchester was the seat of the Saxon kings and the first capital of England. It still is a city with an ambience that sets it apart from other places and its native attractions are being developed year by year for the visitor.

The Clarendon Way covers about 25 miles of fine walking and has many access points along its route. No walker on this path, or on the Test Way, need carry provisions: there are small shops and pubs at places along both routes, with the exception of Inkpen Beacon. Even here you may find an ice-cream van!

The TEST WAY
& The CLARENDON WAY

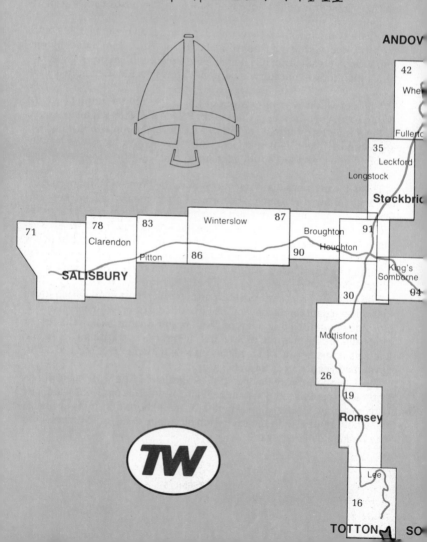

INKPEN BEACON
61
Combe
Linkenholt
60
Hurstbourr
54

ANDOV
42
Whe
Fullerto
35
Leckford
Longstock
Stockbri
87 Winterslow
71
78 Clarendon
83
Pitton 86
90 Broughton
Houghton
91
SALISBURY
King's Somborne
30
94
Mottisfont
26
19
Romsey
Lee
16
TOTTON SO

TW

Contents

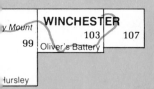

THE TEST WAY
TOTTON TO ROMSEY

The Test near Totton

TOTTON TO ROMSEY

'They are not long rivers — the Test and Itchen — but long enough for men with unfevered blood in their veins to find sweet and peaceful homes on their margins.'

W.H. Hudson, 1903

The Test Way runs for fifty miles from the Hampshire coast to the Berkshire and Wiltshire borders. It runs through some of the finest country in the South, rich with wildlife and natural beauty, and rich with historical, literary and sporting associations.

Danish invaders have gone this way: so have English soldiers returning home, farmers returning from market, nuns and monks, anglers seeking trout — and many others. They have all left their marks and made the Test Valley a unique area for walkers to explore.

The Test Way starts at **Totton**, which lies at the extreme western edge of a conurbation between Southampton and Portsmouth that some have called Solent City.

The Solent is the drowned valley of a great river which once flowed into the Channel from the west, eventually 'bursting its banks' to the south and making the Isle of Wight. Totton stands on the west bank of its largest tributary, the Test. Others included the Stour and the Hampshire Avon.

On the opposite bank is **Southampton**, a city founded on the sea and still strongly dependent on its docks and dockside industries. Like many ports, its fortunes have varied: in broad terms, it thrived during Saxon and medieval times (though on different sites), declined during the 16th century, grew and grew from the early Victorian period to modern times and now, some would say, is declining once more. Recent attempts to breathe new life into Southampton docks have included the creation of a free port area.

During Saxon times the prosperity of Southampton fuelled the growth of Winchester (see p. 102). Then called Hamwih, the port area lay on the west bank of the River Itchen, close to the St Mary's district of the modern city. It is estimated that the town which served the dockside had a population of about 5,000, making it the largest settlement known at this time.

The medieval port lay below what is now the city centre, close to the Eastern Docks, which date from the 1840s. It was from the Ocean Terminal in this part of the docks that such famous liners as the *Queen Mary* and *Queen Elizabeth* once plied in style across the Atlantic, a trade that was killed after the war by the advent of civil air travel.

Today, the *QE2* is an occasional visitor to Southampton, but the world's most magnificent liner, the *Royal Princess*, after a brief visit to

Aerial view of the Test River beyond Southampton Docks

the port for naming before her maiden voyage in 1984, will probably never be seen again in Southampton Water.

Much of Southampton's traffic is in The Western Docks, a single quay more than a mile in length. It is marked by a long line of derricks and dates from the late 1920s. The quay stretches to the most recent of Southampton's dock facilities, the Prince Charles Container Terminal, built in the late 1960s on reclaimed land.

At about the same time a local company set up a small exhibition for boatbuilders. Now called the Southampton International Boat Show, and held each year in September, it has grown to rival its London counterpart.

Allowing for the luxury of modern yachting, many of the boats at the Southampton show are perhaps representative of the size of vessels that have plied the waters of the Solent for centuries. Some of them would have made for the Itchen, while others would have 'beaten up' Southampton Water to Redbridge and the Test.

The estuaries of these two chalk streams, that have achieved a national — and even international — fame, are formally similar but are in fact very different. Take a train from Winchester to Southampton and then on to Romsey and you will see the difference: the lower Itchen valley is quite heavily industrialised, the lower Test is not.

Both rivers are 'gateways to the interior', used by Saxon and Danish invaders and other more peaceful folk, but the Itchen led to Winchester, a capital city, while the Test led to . . . well, let us find out.

Redbridge and the reed bed north of it in the Lower Test Nature Reserve

Before setting out on a journey that passes many mills, we should note that by the sea the mill was often driven by the tide. A working example has been restored at Eling, just below Totton. One snag of this apparently unlimited source of power was that millers had to keep very unsocial hours: the tides were their masters.

Opposite Totton is the **Redbridge** district of Southampton, where timber from the New Forest was loaded onto ships for the Naval dockyards in the 18th and early 19th centuries. It was here also that six experimental ships, designed to conserve stocks of timber, were built in the late 1790s by General Samuel Bentham, brother of the social reformer.

Redbridge has always been an important point for crossing the Test, at least since medieval times, when rights to levy a toll were granted to local men. Alongside the modern road bridge can be seen two earlier constructions, a five-span 17th century bridge and another built in 1793. They spanned a wide estuary flanked by marshland, but were not completely successful. A few years after the 18th century structure had been built William Gilpin, the celebrated vicar of Boldre, described the crossing as 'a long wooden bridge and causeway, sometimes covered by the tide'.

The first leg of the Test Way, soon after its start at the Salmon Leap pub, gives some idea of the formidable barrier posed by the Test. The path strikes out across Ruddy Mead (a name said to be a thousand years old), a winding muddy route across little wooden foot-bridges.

This section of the Test valley is an NCC Site of Special Scientific Interest, part of which has been a nature reserve since 1978. Managed by

the Hampshire and Isle of Wight Naturalists' Trust, the present reserve covers 270 acres and demonstrates three distinct types of estuarine habitat.

In the area immediately above Redbridge is one of the largest expanses of reed bed on the South Coast: it gave its name to the district (Reedbridge) and is cut commercially for thatching materials. Vast numbers of reed and sedge warblers breed here in the summer, while in spring and autumn it becomes a roosting area for such birds as swallows and sand martins.

A small flock of bearded tit, an uncommon species, is usually to be found here in the winter, together with occasional rarities such as the bittern.

The lower reaches of the reserve are regularly flooded with salt water and support a number of uncommon plant species which are able to withstand the brackish conditions. These include wild celery, bulbous foxtail (a grass) and brookweed.

Here, where water is slow to freeze over in hard weather, can also be found a wide variety of wintering birds: redshank, snipe, curlew, dunlin, wigeon, mallard and teal. One particularly rare species which visits the Lower Test for several months in the winter is the water pipit.

Above the brackish grasslands is an area which is unaffected by salt water and was formerly 'floated' as meadow and used to grow hay: some of the old hatches still remain. It supports several species of orchid and the graceful wetland plant, water avens, as well as the common king cup or marsh marigold, found throughout the valley.

Beyond the reserve the Test way crosses to the east side of the valley

and roughly follows the Southampton–Salisbury railway line as far as the M27. Once under the motorway bridge the path comes to the ancient hamlet of **Nursling**.

A short detour worth taking here leads to Northcliffe School, marked **Grove Place** on the map. Instead of turning left after the motorway, turn right: after about two hundred yards there is a view to the left of the school building at the end of a driveway and avenue of mistletoe-hung limes.

Grove Place was a grand Elizabethan country house, built in the middle of the 16th century by James Paget, the son of a wealthy London merchant and alderman. During the period 1813–54 it was used as a private lunatic asylum.

Osbert Crawford, a pioneer of aerial photography and the first Archaeological Officer of the Ordnance Survey, believed that there was evidence in the grounds for a terrace which was the 'north-eastern shore' of Southampton Water at a time when the sea level was higher.

Crawford, who lived nearby, rarely wasted an opportunity: in December 1940, at the height of the Luftwaffe bombing of Southampton, one bomb aimed at a military hutment to the east of Nursling Mill landed harmlessly in the peat nearby. The archaeologist eagerly took a sample and had it dated to 7500–6000 BC, later commenting: 'Thus information that would otherwise have been tedious and difficult was supplied in a moment'.

The path continues west, towards Nursling church. To the north are views of the high lands of Stockbridge Down and Danebury.

Nursling is famous as the site of one of the earliest Christian foundations in Hampshire. It was from the monastery here that St Boniface, who came from Crediton, set out in the 8th century on evangelical missions to what is now Germany, where he is said to be better remembered than in this country. He died there at the hands of a heathen band in 754.

The precise site of the monastery, which was destroyed by the Danes in the late 9th century, is not known, though it may have been close to the present church.

Nursling takes it name from Nutshalling, which appears on a plaque on the Church Room, which was built in 1897, the year of Queen Victoria's Diamond Jubilee. The old name — meaning the nut grove by the water meadows — was in use at least until the 1930s.

A branch of the Roman road between Winchester and Clausentum (now Bitterne, a suburb of Southampton) crossed the Test at Nursling, according to the historian I.D. Margary. Considerable remains of the period were unearthed to the south when ballast for the railway was dug in 1880.

It seems clear that this part of the Test valley has become depopulated, for there are deserted village sites at several places where there are now only isolated dwellings. The path passes close by several of them — Lee, Skidmore and, above Romsey, Roke.

The river between Nursling and Lee, glimpsed from the path, has now lost all signs of its link with the sea. Here it is one stream and not a multiplicity of little streams, as elsewhere. The broad silvery water seen between level banks now looks equal to its reputation as fishing country.

TOTTON TO ROMSEY

Though flat and open to the winds, this is where the salmon fisherman in particular is likely to find his sport.

But talk to any water keeper and he will tell you that salmon fishing on the Test, traditionally limited to the river below Romsey, is in a bad state. Other rivers face similar problems, due to netting in the breeding grounds off Greenland. Whereas the four-mile stretch of water from the M27 to Romsey used to yield 2,000 fish a year, it is now down to a hundred and, as a result, is being stocked as a trout fishery.

Salmon fishing on the Broadlands water seems to date from 1880, when the agent at the time, G.R. Kendle, caught a 14lb fish at a spot below Romsey which is called after him. In *The Ever-Rolling Stream*, which is essential reading for anyone with an interest in this water, the present river keeper, Bernard Aldrich, records how Kendle was so excited he opened the river to other fishermen, for a fee, of course!

The record fish, a monster salmon of 43lbs, nearly four feet long and three feet in girth, was caught two years after Kendle's catch. In the same year, long before the river was threatened by pollution or water abstraction, 4000 salmon fry from the United States were released to keep up stocks.

Yet, whatever the problems, being head keeper on the Broadlands water is clearly a job for life. Since Kendle's original appointment of John Cragg ('a tough man, the scourge of local poachers'), and a short spell by Cragg Junior, there have only been two other men, Walter Geary and Bernard Aldrich, a Londoner, who took over in 1956.

Fishermen who seek Bernard's advice on artificial flies are likely to be told: 'One of my most successful flies was one I tied using a vivid blue feather from my daughter's toy shuttlecock and a blue wool body taken from a sweater my wife was knitting'.

Beyond Lee the Test Way doubles back and follows a causeway over farmland drained by deep cuts. It leads to **Moorcourt Farm** and the River Blackwater, which joins the main stream below Nursling Mill. This substantial tributary rises in Embley Park, Wellow, once the home of Florence Nightingale.

After Moorcourt the path follows the western edge of the valley, snugly tucked in under wooded terraces that rise up in waves. From here to Romsey is delightful walking country with superb views across the valley. Two miles to the east can be seen the distinctive 'plum pudding' of Toot Hill, once the site of a semaphore-type of telegraph station that linked Whitehall and Plymouth.

At the approach to Romsey (pronounced Rumsey by the natives), high up on the shoulder of the valley, is Pauncefoot Hill, which takes it names from the Norman knight to whom the land was granted after the Conquest. During the First World War a remount depot was set up here to serve some of the seven million men who passed through Southampton, Britain's No. 1 Embarkation Port.

Ahead in the distance, surmounted by an octagonal wooden belfry, is the tower of Romsey Abbey, which dominated the town during the middle ages. Closer at hand, glimpsed through the trees to the east, is **Broadlands House**, the home of the late Lord Louis Mountbatten. A fine view of the house beside the river is seen as the Test Way reaches

Reproduced from the
Ordnance Survey
Pathfinder Map

Middlebridge on the edge of the town.

There has been a grand house on the Broadlands site since the middle of the 16th century. After two centuries in the hands of the St Barbe family, the original Tudor and Jacobean manor house passed briefly to Humphrey Sydenham, whose ruin in the South Sea Bubble obliged him to sell up. In 1736, therefore, Broadlands was bought by Henry Temple, 1st Viscount Palmerston, and has been passed down ever since. The present owner, Lord Romsey, is the grandson of Lord Mountbatten, who married into the estate.

The mid-Georgian Palladian-style mansion and landscaped grounds that we see now date from 1767–80, when 'Capability Brown' and his son-in-law Henry Holland transformed the manor house into one of the finest stately homes in the country.

Since 1979, two months before Lord Mountbatten's assassination at the hands of IRA bombers, Broadlands has been open to the public. One of its finely furnished rooms houses a special display of Broadland's other famous owner, the prime minister Lord Palmerston.

The life of Lord Louis himself is displayed outside the house in a stable block. A great-grandson of Queen Victoria, Mountbatten had a distinguished career, particularly as Supreme Commander South-East Asia in Burma and as the last Viceroy of India to serve before the independence of that country.

ROMSEY
TO
STOCKBRIDGE

The Test River

ROMSEY TO STOCKBRIDGE

'Romsey in the mud,
Southampton on the stones,
Winchester eats the meat,
Andover picks the bones.'

Traditional, quoted by Telford Varley in *Hampshire*, 1909

Romsey is an 'island', a patch of firm ground, surrounded by water. Only skilful engineering and centuries of containment have kept the water in convenient places as it struggles towards the sea. Yet without it Romsey would not have prospered.

The town's position astride the braids of the Test made it a mill town. Until modern times there were mills for fulling cloth and grinding corn, for making paper, parchment and leather board, as well as other waterside processes such as brewing and tanning.

The roots of these industries were in the abbey, founded in the 10th century by the Saxon King, Edward the Elder, with his daughter Aelflaeda as abbess. If time allows, a detour from the Test Way into the centre of Romsey to see the abbey is well worth while.

Romsey Abbey was a Benedictine monastery for nuns which in its early years had strong royal connections and attracted ladies from some of the wealthiest families in the land. They and their pupils and their retinues brought trade and prosperity to the town.

Fairs and markets were held in the 'square' in the centre of Romsey, now marked by a bronze statue of Palmerston. Inspection of the street plan shows how the through roads, which originally ran towards the river crossing at the Middlebridge, acquired a dog-leg as they drifted towards the market place.

In the middle ages the abbey ruled the town and held extensive lands to the east of the Test, stretching to a stream called the Fishlake. One arm of this waterway, a former mill stream called Abbey Water, is met at the Memorial Park as the town is entered from the Test Way via Middlebridge and Saddlers Mill.

The present abbey church was started in about 1120 and is widely regarded as one of the finest Norman churches in Britain. In fact, its architecture shows several styles, the pure Norman of the east end merging with later phases of building to the west.

In its later years the monastery declined: its nuns were often rebuked at visitations for 'scandals' that ranged from spending the night outside the precincts of the convent to staying in bed too late! At the dissolution the abbey church survived and was sold to the people because it was the town's parish church. The convent buildings, which spread to the south, were however swept away, though in 1976 the refectory was discovered in the Close under a later facade.

St Barbe family memorial in Romsey Abbey

Restoration of the abbey church owes a great deal to the energy of one of the most eccentric vicars to have held the living at Romsey, the Rev. Edward Berthon. Following a local tradition that the great abbey could never be kept warm, many of the arches inside were filled with 'hundreds of cartloads of bricks and all kind of rubbish' as a crude form of space-filling and insulation. Berthon condemned the idea as 'humbug' and, with the support of Lord Palmerston, had the church cleared in 1845.

One problem created by this process was that two stained-glass windows on the east side of the retro-choir had 'their heads cut off' by the cleared arches and needed to be lowered. Attempts to raise funds to have the work done professionally failed, so Berthon decided to do the job himself. With the aid of four labourers deliberately chosen for their *lack* of skill, he cut out masonry and resited the huge windows by means of a clever winching system that involved 'four powerful screws of two-inch round iron'.

Berthon, who was clearly fascinated by technology, claimed to have invented the screw propellor. He was best known, however, for designing collapsible boats, which 'the Berthon Boat Company' built from canvas and wood and tested at Romsey. Amongst the advantages of these craft was that they were portable and, as lifeboats, needed very little storage space.

Several passenger ships used boats built according to Berthon's ideas: it was their failure on one of them, the recently located *Titanic*, which in 1912 eventually scuppered the cleric's invention, though by this time he was dead.

There is a display on Berthon's life to the east of the abbey, in Church Court, in a medieval building called **King John's House**. It is a much-patched brick and flint building with roof timbers strangely poking out of the eaves and was of no particular interest until 1927, when the top of an Early English window (still clearly visible) was spotted above the later extension.

A detailed inspection revealed that the house was probably a royal hunting lodge. In particular, the original plaster revealed crude engravings of the arms of knights who may have accompanied Edward I when he stayed in the town on the night of 13th February 1306.

In recent times Romsey has become known as the home of Strong's brewery: throughout Hampshire and south of England its beer is advertised by means of an almost childlike painting of the countryside, accompanied by the motto 'You are in the Strong Country'. This was the brainchild of banker and publisher David Faber, who in the 1880s bought up three small breweries, reorganised them and gave them a 'brand image'.

Alas, beer is no longer brewed in Romsey, though the site beside the Fishlake — now owned by Whitbread's — can be seen to the north of the abbey in the Horsefair.

Returning to the Market Place, an interesting relic of the Civil War can be seen on the north side of what is now the Romsey Working Men's Conservative Club. On the building is a large wrought iron bracket from which in 1644 two Roundhead soldiers were hanged by their own officers for murder.

When the war was over the Protector's son, Richard Cromwell, used to come to Romsey from his home at Hursley, near Winchester, to worship with dissenters. At the entrance to Abbey Meads, which runs between the Market Place and the Memorial Park, is a United Reform church which owes its congregational beginnings in 1662 to one of the preachers that Richard came to hear, Thomas Warren. Formerly rector of Houghton (see p. 93), Mr Warren — in common with many other clerics at the time — was stripped of his living for refusing to accept the Prayer Book, which had been restored by the Act of Uniformity.

The United Reform church has a distinctive little turret which is visible some way from the town.

A much more pragmatic man of this period, the Romsonian Sir William Petty (1623–87), achieved great wealth and rank from humble beginnings and was also an original member of the Royal Society. One stroke of luck which befell him during a period teaching anatomy at Oxford was the recovery of a hanged murderess called Anne Green. Expecting to find a cadaver in the dissecting room, he instead found the criminal to be still alive. As well as giving 'proof' of his skills as a physician, this bizarre episode enabled him to 'recover expenses' by exhibiting the unfortunate woman.

The route back to the Test Way passes Saddlers Mill, built in 1748 and now provided with a salmon leap, and then goes between two houses to a footpath fork; the way continues to the right.

Below the mill is the outlet of the Horsefair branch of the Fishlake. At one time the water from this stream was so 'rich' (tradition blames a butcher's offal) that fish grew fat at its outlet, one rod-caught specimen reaching 19 lbs!

The way continues up the west side of the Test towards **Squabb Wood**.

Squabb Wood

It crosses small streams over simple plank bridges (though Broadlands water keeper Bernard Aldrich points out that these may cost more than £1000) and enters woodland reminiscent of the New Forest. There are oak, beech, birch and silver birch: squirrels streak up the branches and underneath are holly and rhododendron.

Alder grows in boggy bottoms from which small dark streams start their journey to the Test. It is, of course, a deceptively natural habitat managed by foresters.

After Squabb Wood the path passes close to **Stanbridge Earls**, the site of a deserted moated hamlet. It then skirts **Awbridge**, a village which contains a remarkable number of springs and a huge ornamental lake in the grounds of Awbridge Danes, a house which takes its name from a Danish encampment that was made nearby.

Traces of the incursions of the Danes in the 10th and 11th centuries are found in a number of places along the Test, which provided these invaders with a convenient entrance to the hinterland. From time to time over a long period they wintered at Southampton and were 'bought off' with the customary Danegeld. The monastery at Nursling, as already mentioned, was destroyed and Romsey, too, was threatened, forcing the abbess and her community to flee to Winchester.

The fiercest fighting followed the massacre of St Brice's Day, 13th November 1002, when Ethelred ordered the killing of Danes who had settled in the country. The revenge of the Danish king, Sweyn, was truly terrible and many Hampshire people suffered greatly.

From the higher land beyond Awbridge Farm is a superb view of the valley of the Test — which is now quite wide — across to the high lands

of Braishfield and Parnholt Wood. In the midst of this rich landscape is the Southampton–Salisbury railway line, which has been with us since the start of the walk. But it carries only a light traffic and soon, at **Kimbridge**, we leave it for good. Here the Test is joined by the Dun, a small tributary which runs under Dean Hill and drains lands extending into Wiltshire. Until recently it was a river without a name — or to be precise, with a variety of names, including Blackwater, Whitewater, and Rife.

It was also called the Barge River, after the canal which in 1802 was opened between Alderbury Common on the outskirts of Salisbury and Kimbridge. Traces of the former waterway can be seen as the path crosses the Dun. It was intended to link the Avon with the Test, to connect Salisbury with Southampton via Redbridge by means of 15 locks, but it was never completed at either end. Within a few years it had been abandoned by commercial traffic and an ambitious plan to enter Southampton via a tunnel half a mile in length was never completed.

Kimbridge later became a railway junction where the Test Valley line from Andover (p. 45) met the present line. Before the path crosses the Dun, the line of the Andover track can be seen curving across to the opposite bank of the river, where it ran north under prominent white cliffs at Lower Brook.

The Test at Kimbridge, which is noticeably clearer than at Romsey, is a famous trout water. The Dun is also well known by trout fishermen, not particularly for its fishing but as a source of river insects, which were used in the 1890s to restock the Houghton Club fisheries upstream. It was particularly noted for mayfly by Rev. Richard Durnford, the Chilbolton cleric whose diaries, first published in 1911, have become a minor classic of early 19th century fishing literature.

After Kimbridge the Test Way passes through **Mottisfont** to the north, coming into the village at the church, past a small burial ground given in the Queen's Jubilee year, 1977, by Mr Charles Hamblen-Thomas, a local ENT surgeon.

One of the most unusual features of Mottisfont church and its chapels is that they were for centuries attached to the see of York. This reflects the fact that they were founded by Wilfred, a great churchman of the North whose tumultuous life included spells in York separated by long periods of exile. In 677 he was deprived of his bishopric by King Ecgfrith of Northumbria and forced to seek the support of the pope: the King, it seems, was miffed by Wilfred's success in encouraging his first wife to swap a wordly life for a religious one.

At a time when pagan beliefs were still being supplanted by Christiantity, Wilfred founded a new see at Selsey, near Chichester, and may also have been granted the former Roman fort at Porchester, near Portsmouth. He also turned his attention to the West Saxon kingdom outside the seven-mile radius of the see of Winchester and built a church at Mottisfont. When he was reinstated as Archbishop of York in 686 Mottisfont church therefore became attached to that see, and remained so until the dissolution.

Nearly five hundred years later Mottisfont was again involved in a similar affair. William, Bishop of York and a nephew of King Stephen, also had to flee south, when his uncle lost control of his kingdom. For

Mottisfont Abbey

eleven years he lived in Winchester and during this time, it is believed, helped to rebuild the church at Mottisfont: the nave certainly dates from this period, though the chancel is 13th century. It is a beautiful intimate little church with a huge Norman chancel arch and more 15th century glass than in any other Hampshire village church, according to Pevsner and Lloyd.

Amongst the memorials is one to Daniel Meinertzhagen (1875–98) whose family came from Bremen and settled in Mottisfont: the tablet incorporates a stone carving from a chapel built in that city by a forebear in 1693.

In the middle ages Mottisfont was well known to pilgrims, for one of the principal routes between Winchester and Salisbury crossed the Test nearby at Kimbridge. As a result the priory in the village thrived on providing food and drink for weary travellers — in return for indulgences. Indeed, that was probably one of the main reasons that the site was chosen by Austin canons when at the beginning of the 13th century William de Briwere, a prominent Hampshire landowner, founded **Mottisfont Abbey**, as it is now called.

The priory prospered, as recorded in a detailed 'rental' prepared by a cellarer in about 1343 and now held by the Hampshire Record Office. Two mills were powered by a spring, which still pours out 200 gallons of crystal clear water per minute. There were gardens, orchards, a tannery, dove houses and all the other accoutrements of a wealthy self-sufficient community. And there was land, extending over a fair area of Hampshire and Wiltshire and including property in Winchester.

This happy scene was shattered by the Black Death and the priory never recovered. At one stage the number of canons was reduced to three, assisted by the usual complement of lay brethren.

The present building, which is National Trust property, is architecturally schizophrenic. To the south it appears to be a grand 18th century country house, which it was, while to the north it shows distinct traces of a large 12th/13th century church, which it was also. The newer facade was built for Sir Richard Mill in 1743 and it is something of a miracle that so much of the priory church was retained.

The building also survived an earlier Tudor facelift, when it was acquired at the dissolution (incidentally, in return for the villages of Chelsea and Paddington) by William 1st Lord Sandys, the Lord Chamberlain of the day. Mottisfont was clearly a 'second home' for an old man in search of seclusion, for Lord Sandys already possessed the Vyne, a Tudor mansion near Basingstoke, also owned by the National Trust. During the alterations he stayed with the rector but did not live to see the work completed.

Mottisfont Abbey remained in the Lord Chamberlain's family until 1934, when it was bought by Mr Gilbert Russell. He and his wife laid out the splendid gardens that can now be seen and also commissioned Rex Whistler to create the 'Gothic *trompe-l'oeil* fantasy' in the saloon which now bears his name. Perhaps the most effective illusion is that of the 'smoking urn', painted flat but looking real enough to touch!

Mottisfont is also noted for its historic roses — including the ancestral roses of York and Lancaster — which were planted in 1972–3 by Graham

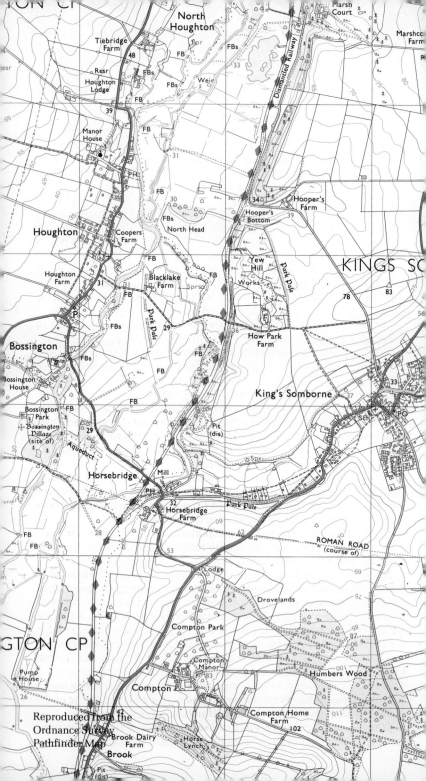

Thomas and represent 40 years of collecting on his part.

There is a fine view of the abbey as the Test Way crosses towards Oakley Farm and the east bank of the river. The large red-brick building seen to the right of the mansion is a stable block built in 1836 to satisfy the needs of its hunter-cleric owner, Sir John Barker-Mill.

The path makes for the white cliffs of **Lower Brook**, parts of which are still worked for chalk. Here the valley is as peaceful as anywhere: houses nestle under the cliffs and summer houses stand in the fields in a quiet, sheltered, balmy atmosphere. It was not always like this, as the former track of the **Test Valley Railway** indicates.

At Lower Brook the path takes to the old route of the line and stays with it until Fullerton, ten miles away, where the track continued its way to Andover, along the valley of the Anton, a tributary of the Test. It was the demise of this line in Beeching's 'dissolution of the railways' in the 1960s that prompted the signposting of the Test Way.

However, it must be admitted that walking along former railway routes is not to everyone's taste. Much has been done — and is still being done — by the Hampshire County Council to improve the path by grassing it and encouraging it to 'wind about a bit'.

There are alternatives for this section of the walk, on the west bank of the river, including a diversion to the hillfort at Danebury to the north, via North Houghton (see p. 92). But the former railway track does have the great advantage that it runs on the quiet side of the valley: because the river runs so close under the cliffs to the east, all the settlements along this part of the Test stand on the opposite side.

The Test Valley Railway was opened in 1865 and in more senses than one replaced a canal that ran between Andover and Redbridge: it was built over the top of it, and literally left its scars on the valley hereabouts. All along the path can be seen white gashes in the cliffs where, it is said, chalk was excavated to fill the old waterway.

At **Horsebridge** one of the old stations still stands and is being converted into a private house. It is the sort of station where you can imagine the guard holding up the train when he saw someone running up the road and porters kept a fire burning in the waiting room.

Horsebridge was for centuries an important point for crossing the Test. It was somewhere here that the Roman road from Winchester crossed on its way to Old Sarum (see p. 94).

The path continues alongside the Park Stream, which presumably takes it name either from How Park or the nearby deer park, once owned by John of Gaunt (see p. 95). It soon crosses the Clarendon Way and then enters a stretch which is locally renowned for its bird life. The thick hedges and patches of woodland that line the path almost to Stockbridge provide an ideal habitat for many species of small birds — warblers, tits and finches. Equally, the water meadows and marshlands of the Test are here frequented by a rich variety of waterfowl.

Birdwatchers from the Somborne and District Society have recorded a large number of species in the woodland hereabouts, including chiffchaff, blackcap, willow warbler, bullfinch, redshank, yellow hammer, nightingale and turtle dove. Reed and sedge warblers breed on the large private lake that lies to the west of the path near Marsh Court: it is also

31

The old railway station at Horsebridge

Marsh Court

a wintering site for gadwall and a place where such birds as snipe, kestrel, sparrowhawk and the occasional hobby may be seen. In 1976 the marsh harrier is thought to have attempted to breed on the lake.

Glimpsed through the hedge, Marsh Court Lake is a private world of waving reed, honking geese and squawking duck: it is said to be full of large pike.

Marsh Court itself is a grand white house with towering chimneys perched on a hill in a spot where the cliffs temporarily fall back to the east. Now used as a prep school, the house is the work of the famous architect Sir Edwin Lutyens. He designed it at the turn of the century for Herbert Johnson, 'a typically Edwardian adventurer, stock jobber and sportsman'.

The walls are made of chalk clunch, 'a whim which speculators have taken up here and there and always disastrously', comments Pevsner and Lloyd. The gardens were laid out on several levels in an elaborate plan devised by Gertrude Jekyll and have recently been restored by the Hampshire Gardens Trust.

Stretching along the west side of the Test Way from Marsh Court Lake to the edge of Stockbridge is an 80-acre patch of pasture with a special significance: it is common land with grazing rights held by the burgesses of the Borough of Stockbridge. Moreover, this ancient right is still administered each year in manorial courts held in the town.

The common, together with the lordship of the manor of Stockbridge, have been vested in the National Trust since 1946, though the quondam lady of the manor, historian Miss Rosalind Hill, still presides over the courts of baron and leet, which are often attended by interested visitors. Each year in March, after the proceedings have been opened by the town crier, the steward swears in those who have been called to act on the jury.

Officials are appointed, including a bailiff and sergeant of the mace, and details of the marsh are discussed, such as opening and closing dates for grazing. A recent court decided to sponsor a 'ragwort pull' to improve the pasture without the use of weed killers.

The survival of these ancient courts, which owe their authority to charters of 1190 and 1200, is due to Miss Hill's father, Sir Norman Hill, who revived them in 1923 after buying the lordship of the manor. The title lay as an unredeemed pledge with a London pawnbroker, and the courts had not sat since 1880, though miraculously the 17th century silver mace which dignifies the proceedings, had been preserved by a former steward.

Stockbridge Down, a large area of common downland to the east of the town, was also donated to the National Trust in 1946 at the same time as the marsh.

The Test Way, keeps close to the former railway track, as it skirts the edge of Stockbridge, but the town and its main street (the two are virtually the same) are well worth seeing. Some walkers may, however, wish to take a detour to the ancient earthwork of **Danebury**, which lies to the north-west of the town.

One way of reaching this famous site, as already mentioned, is to cross the river at Horsebridge or How Park and walk up the west bank to North

Mill at Horsebridge

Houghton. Thereafter, a footpath via Houghton Down Farm and Shepherd's Bush leads to Danebury Down. Other alternatives include walking through Stockbridge and taking a footpath to Houghton Down Farm or reaching the site from the Test Way to the north, turning west at Atners Hill towards Longstock and a path that leads under Blackstake Hill.

The path to Danebury about 2000–2500 years ago would have passed through a landscape of small farms, with fields of corn and barley and a few animals. The hillfort, faced by its eastern neighbour at Woolbury, would have been the dominant feature of the area, physically, socially and spiritually — rather like an African kraal township. Its main role would have been as a centre where grain and wool were exchanged for manufactured and other goods obtained from other regions or made in the fort.

Though this picture of Iron Age life by the Test is almost certainly only 'half true', it is based on the sound evidence of fifteen seasons of archaeological excavation under the direction of Professor Barry Cunliffe. Modern archaeologists are now able to decipher a good deal of the fine details of the past and Danebury is one of the sites where these new techniques have been applied to the full.

It all started in 1968 when Professor Cunliffe and the County Land Agent for Hampshire, Colin Bonsey, visited Danebury one afternoon in March. The beech trees which covered the site were dying and had to be replaced: it was an ideal opportunity to dig, refill and replant an area which had never properly been excavated. To test the idea that 'developed' hillforts were more than mere centres of refuge, as previously thought, it was decided to strip large areas of the inside of the site as

Danebury ✓

well as cutting through the three ramparts.

Today Danebury is still an impressive earthwork, particularly the massive eastern gateway and the long ditch that runs for a kilometre to the east. For many years visitors have watched as volunteer diggers with trowel and brush have uncovered a complex pattern of indentations and holes in the chalk. In his book *Danebury*, Barry Cunliffe likens the result of each season's dig to 'a slab of Gruyere cheese'!

Central to the purpose of Danebury, which possibly had its own 'king', are the 5000 storage pits which are estimated to lie beneath the turf. Many of these are shaped like a bee skep, with a large volume and a narrow entrance, and were filled with grain and then tightly sealed with clay. This made the pits self-sterilising, as initial fermentation of the grain quickly used up the oxygen within and produced carbon dioxide.

It is estimated that the amount of grain which could be stored at Danebury was about twenty times that required by the estimated population of 200–350. This enhanced capacity, together with such activities as metal-working and weaving, probably enabled the people to obtain such commodities as amber, glass and bronze from distant communities, Professor Cunliffe has concluded.

But this 'trade' did not involve money; rather it was an 'embedded economy' in which nobles and aristocrats exchanged gifts.

Life at Danebury seems to have been quite stable over a period of five hundred years, from 600 BC. Traces of houses found on the site suggest that some of the people lived in double-skinned structures for added warmth. The walls were made from wattle daubed with clay, which was probably obtained from Tertiary deposits to the south and stored in pits.

The people of Danebury ate mainly barely or wheat with a wide variety of other foodstuffs, including honey and horse meat. Sheep, cattle and pigs were useful as a 'store of protein' and provided wool, hides and other materials to use in exchange with distant groups.

One important point which Professor Cunliffe emphasises is that Iron Age life was governed by ritual and spiritual observances similar to those recorded for Celtic Ireland. Indeed, traces of structures which could have been shrines — they were similar in plan to some Romano-British temples — have been found at Danebury, while the storage pits often contained 'special animal burials', sometimes involving ravens, a bird of symbolic significance.

The end at Danebury came suddenly, in about 100 BC, at which time the great inner gate was burnt. No one knows why, but it was a common fate of hillforts in Southern England, probably in response to the 'bow wave' of increasing Roman power in Gaul. The old way of life was abruptly 'transformed into a capitalist-based system of trade motivated by highly efficient Roman entrepreneurs'.

The collapse of Danebury was probably akin to the fall of native societies in modern times in the face of European exploration.

The excavations at Danebury have also uncovered more recent features, including artificial warrens dating from the early 17th century. To make the task of rearing and catching rabbits as easy as possible, warreners dug trenches in the chalk and constructed a system of burrows with known entrances and exits.

STOCKBRIDGE
TO
WHERWELL

Fishermans Hut near Longstock

STOCKBRIDGE TO WHERWELL

'Stockbridge is the most famous of the world's fisheries.'

John Waller Hills, 1946

Game for sale, the Market Room of the Grosvenor Hotel, Stokes's roadside garage with its 'Toad-era' petrol cans, antiques, the Town Hall ('very elementary and without graces' — Pevsner and Lloyd), places to sup and fishing — all these make **Stockbridge** a high spot on the Test Way.

Despite being on the main roads between London and Salisbury and Winchester and Salisbury, Stockbridge is as close to an unspoilt country town as you will find. It was a medieval 'new town' and was founded in about 1200 as 'the street of King's Somborne' by the lord of the manor, William de Briwere. It rests on an ancient chalk causeway which enables travellers to cross the seven streams which make up the Test at this point. The town still is awash with water: little runnels flow in channels between the houses and alongside and under the street.

The main arm of the river is at the western end of the High Street and has been crossed by a bridge since at least the middle of the 15th century. The present modern structure bears an enigmatic inscription which gives credit to earlier builders, 'John Gylinges, otherwise said Lokke, and Richard Gater, and Margaret the wife of the aforesaid John and Richard'. Presumably Margaret married twice.

Near the bridge, about a hundred yards along the turning to Houghton, is a house with another baffling inscription, in Welsh! This is the equivalent of a 'B & B' sign, painted to attract the custom of Welsh drovers who passed through Stockbridge, presumably on their way to Winchester. The translation is alluring: 'Seasonal Hay — Tasty Pastures — Good Beer — Comfortable Beds'.

Although trade of this kind, and markets and fairs, provided Stockbridge with a living for most of its history, for the past century or so it has been best known for its fishing and its horse-racing.

One relic of the racing is Hermit Lodge, a house which stands opposite the Drovers House and takes its name from a local horse which won the 1877 Derby in a snowstorm at odds of a hundred to one.

The main racecourse, which lay between the high lands of Danebury Down and Chattis Hill and the river, was used between 1753 and 1898, generally for two days in June. In the early 19th century there was also racing on Houghton Down and Stockbridge Down.

For nearly 70 years the Danebury course was used by the Bibury Club, a famous institution of the turf. In 1850, for example, there were eight races on the card.

Stockbridge

One of the leading trainers was John Day, who in 1831 built a grandstand for the Danebury course, the remains of which can still be seen. He had stables at Houghton Down but it was his stables at Danebury which became a legend in the sport. From here came three winners of the Derby, four winners of the Oaks, four winners of the Two Thousand Guineas and one winner of the St Leger.

John Day was followed at Danebury by another famous trainer, Tom Cannon. The jockey Lester Piggott can trace his roots to these men and Stockbridge. At its peak the area had no less than nine racing stables. One of these, at Chattis Hill, survives and is now used by a riding school.

Racing at Stockbridge, which always had something of the informality of point-to-point, eventually died out as better transport made it possible for spectators to travel to courses such as those at Newmarket and Ascot, which had enclosed stands and charged an entrance fee. The town's other sport of fishing has, however, survived — and in great style.

The Royal Yacht Squadron at Cowes is to yachting what the Houghton Club at Stockbridge is to fly fishing. The club rooms at the Grosvenor Hotel at Stockbridge are the mecca of game fishing and the nearby river beats have been at the centre of almost all advances in the sport (and not a few disagreements!).

Writing in 1934, and looking back to the 1880s, a celebrated angling author, John Waller Hills, captures in *River Keeper* the atmosphere of gentlemen fishing the Test in two different periods: 'There was none of the scramble which obtains now, members rushing down on Friday just

Pits (dis)

Tumulus

Cowdown Farm Buildings

Cow Down

Wismore Copse

Cole's Copse

Harew Fores

Pit (dis)

Cowdown Farmhouse

106

Popple Hill Copse

Furzy Croft Copse

Pits (dis)

87

79

Hartway Cops

Tumulus

Pits (dis)

Augurs Hill Copse

DWORTH CLATFORD CP

78

93

Park Brow Copse

Park Farm

82

Keeper's Cottage

Upping Copse

102

105

Hassock Copse

B 3420

Whitehouse

Pit (dis)

Pit (dis)

98

Pit (dis)

New Barn

66

Windwhistle Cottage

73

Dismantled Railway

MS

Sch

FBs

Tumulus

FB

Pit (dis)

Mackrel's Down

FB

MS

B 3420

46

P

Wherwell

Lodge

FB

Red Hill

90

Priory

FB

FB

48

65

Wallis Bottom

86

Pit (dis)

FB

Manor House

FBs

Reservoir

Old Canal

FBs

LL CP

Spr

River Test

Pit (dis)

Chilbolton Common

42

FB

FB

Pit (dis)

PO

Pit (dis)

95

esr

River Anton

43

Dismtd Rly

Cottonworth Farm

Cottonworth

Chilbolton

73

Fullerton

Mill

Fullerton Grange

FBs

FBs

Testcombe

Sewage Works

Test Valley

Thorn

in time for the evening rise and motoring off early on Monday morning. The club came down in a body, a gathering of friends; they came in April for the grannom [a type of fly], and in May for the Mayfly.'

The Houghton Club, which has a small limited membership, was founded in 1822 at a time when the fame of the Test as a trout water was relatively slight. Writing a few years later in *Rural Rides*, William Cobbett praises the river's trout but is equally fulsome about its eels. Indeed, the early club members were mainly interested in fishing for pike and other coarse fish, which are now ruthlessly exterminated.

For a period the club was dominated by a Dr Wickham of Winchester but as its reputation increased it attracted wealthy sportsmen from London and elsewhere. They set out to dedicate this part of the Test to fishing, and in particular to fishing with the dry fly. The neat park-like appearance of much of the river, with benches and thatched fishing huts, is their doing. Moreover, back at the Grosvenor Hotel, or in their studies, these men took a scholarly interest in their sport.

One member in particular is widely regarded as the most influential fisherman of his generation: his name is F. M. Halford. When he came to the Test in 1877 he was so disappointed at his showing with the dry fly that he decided to make a detailed study of the river, its fish and their habits, and the insects on which they feed.

Halford's meticulous attention to detail, by which he sought to create artificial flies that were 'a fairly accurate imitation' of the natural insect, gave a new purpose to fishing and created a fashion which dominated the Test. Moreover, this scientific approach was taken up by others who imbued it with a rather snobbish attitude, according to which dry-fly fishing was the *only* proper way to catch trout.

Today such purism lingers on, but most game fishermen accept that the idea of exact imitation may be irrelevant to the 'fish's-eye view' and that catching fish with nymphs or wet flies is acceptable.

In parallel with Halford's development of dry-fly fishing the last decades of the last century saw improvements in the management of the Test as a prime trout water. In his classic book *A Summer on the Test*, John Waller Hills calls Stockbridge 'the home of scientific management'. He was referring in particular to the work of the Houghton waterman William Lunn, whose life he recorded in the book already mentioned, *River Keeper*. It is a real-life fairy tale.

Lunn, a Londoner by birth, faced a tough childhood after the loss of his father in the Channel en route to a new life in North America. At the age of 12 he decided to run away and became a keeper's boy on a Surrey estate. During a 'curious interlude' as a messenger at a London bank, Lunn was spotted by Herbert Norman, secretary of the Houghton Club, and in 1886 at the age of 24 became his personal attendant. For the rest of his life he lived in a cottage beside Sheepbridge Shallow, Houghton — and he clearly loved it!

Although William Lunn had duties out of season, there was plenty of time to devote to other things, and by all accounts he did not waste it. During his 45 years with the Houghton Club he faithfully observed the river and its life and carried out careful experiments to extend his knowledge. His aim was that of any keeper: to preserve the stock of trout in the river and to make sure that there was plenty of fly. For twenty-six years he battled against a dwindling population of Mayfly, eventually witnessing its return in the 1920s.

Lunn used a number of novel conservation techniques. For example, he invented a method for transplanting insect eggs by the million by coating them onto glass discs, which he then hung in the river. He also invented that stand-by of many fisheries, the fly-board. This derived from his careful observations of the life history of the ephemeridae, which taught him that females often lay their eggs on a solid object such as a post, where they are eaten by caddis crawling up from the bottom. He reasoned that a floating plank of wood would provide a platform that would be out of reach of such predators.

Despite careful conservation the fishing on the Test has, nonetheless, declined. At the beginning of the last century, if records are to be believed, men would sometimes take twenty or forty brace of trout at a session, some of them up to 5lbs in weight.

The Test Way continues from Stockbridge to **Leckford**, at first by the side of the A30 and A3057 and then along the former railway track. It passes under Atner's Tower, a castellated structure which presumably gave its name to the large house nearby.

The path passes under a bridge that carries a road to Longstock: the steeple of the church is visible across the marshes. In recent years this beautiful village has been put on the map by Geoffrey Snagge, who published his view of life in the Test valley in *Letters from Longstock* and a sequel published in 1971. Mr Snagge worked for many years for the John Lewis Partnership, whose founder, John Spelan Lewis, took a strong liking to this part of Hampshire: the water gardens which he created at Longstock are famous.

The entire village of Leckford, which is soon reached, was bought by John Lewis in 1928 and is now owned by the Partnership. It provides fishing, golf and a holiday camp for many partners (not called employees, note) from John Lewis stores all over the country. There is also a 4000-acre farm, said to be the first in the country to work to a five-day week.

Leckford church is a rather dumpy patched-up sort of structure that is perhaps typical of many country churches before the era of Victorian restoration. In the church are what may be the remnants of a cloister belonging to the hospital of the nunnery that is said to have been at Leckford.

From the path at Leckford there is a superb view of the Test valley, looking across to Longstock, with Hazel Down beyond. The meadows are grazed by sheep and contain pens for rearing pheasants and nurseries for raising trout.

Above Leckford the main river moves to the eastern edge of its valley and is joined by the Anton, a substantial tributary which rises above Andover. The path passes through Testcombe bridge, under the road to Goodworth Clatford and Andover, and then climbs **West Down**, an area administered as a public open space by the HCC.

As well as being an important confluence, there was once a railway junction hereabouts and it was here also that the **Andover canal** crossed

William Lunn, famous Stockbridge riverkeeper

from the west bank of the Anton to the east bank of the Test.

The canal was opened in 1794 to enable the produce of Andover to reach the port of Southampton. It was entirely separate from the main river as far as Redbridge at the head of Southampton Water. Unusually, its authorising Act limited activity by specifying the maximum size of barge and hours of use. It was never a financial success, though it continued to be used until 1857, when a railway was built along its route. This eventually became the Andover and Redbridge Railway, which in many places ran over the filled-in canal bed.

Locally called the 'Sprat and Winkle Line', the railway opened in 1865 after a tortuous birth which resulted in it being owned by the London and South-Western Railway. It joined the Salisbury–Southampton line at Kimbridge (see p. 27) and in addition to having a station at Fullerton, near Testcombe, it had stations at Andover, Clatford, Stockbridge, Horsebridge and Mottisfont.

Fullerton became a railway junction in 1885 when the Andover line was joined by another from Hurstbourne that ran via stations at Longparish and Wherwell (both on the Test Way) and was formally called the Northern and Southern Junction Railway. Nicknamed for some reason 'The Nile', this little piece of line ran through some of the quietest country in Hampshire. Its rationale was complicated, but essentially it was built by the LSWR to protect its routes to the South Coast in the face of competition from a new line that ran to Southampton via Didcot and Newbury.

The Hurstbourne-Fullerton route was never, however, a success.

45

STOCKBRIDGE TO WHERWELL

Railway historians say that it was virtually redundant from the start and became little more than a bypass line for the main LSWR line between Basingstoke and Southampton.

In 1927 'The Nile' experienced a brief period of fame when a section near Longparish was taken over by Piccadilly Pictures for scenes in the first film version of that famous play *Ghost Train*. The busiest time for the line, however, was in the last war, when it serviced an RAF ammunition dump set up in Harewood Forest in 1942 in preparation for D-Day. Fullerton station was also pressed into service as offices for the bombed-out Southampton Docks and Marine Authority.

By the early 1950s traffic on the line was fading fast, with trains being cut back to one a day and then two a week. The end came in 1956 when the last goods train pulled out of Longparish station. The Sprat and Winkle line, however, continued until the fall of Dr Beeching's axe in the early 1960s.

Beyond Fullerton the Test Way climbs West Down. In 1934, when the status of this area of land was obscure, threats to enclose it were only prevented by vigorous local protest, conducted from his sick bed by the chairman of the parish council, Alfred Pembroke.

In Taverner's *The Common Lands of Hampshire*, an elderly shepherd recalls that the down was important for the furze that grew on it: this was cut and collected by local people and kept in a handy pile in the fireplace. It was ideal, apparently, for raising a quick blaze to bring a kettle to the boil.

There are fine views from the top of West Down, back towards Stockbridge or west along the Anton valley, where the tributary has carved its way under Makrel's Down. The main river winds its way south across a flat-bottomed valley scattered with patches of woodland and willows leaning at crazy angles.

The Test Way descends towards **Chilbolton**, but skirts the main village on its way to Wherwell. Chilbolton is, however, one of the largest villages in the Test valley and a place of substantial interest.

Like many communities Chilbolton was involved in the events which eventually led to improvements in the lot of the rural poor. Thus, a young plough-boy from Chilbolton was almost hanged after the Swing Riots of 1830, when farm workers destroyed machinery and burned ricks as a protest against low wages. At the last moment the boy's sentence was commuted to transportation for life.

When Joseph Arch, founder of the National Agricultural Labourers Union, toured the British countryside he visited the valleys of the Test and Bourne. He came to Chilbolton in 1876 and addressed a crowd of more than a thousand beside the road between the village and Testcombe bridge.

Beyond West Down the path continues to **Chilbolton Common**, a wild patch of grassland that has an international reputation with botanists, who have found more than a hundred species of grasses and other plants growing there. It is also an important nesting site for snipe, redshank and other birds.

WHERWELL
TO
HURSTBOURNE TARRANT

Wherwell village before 1914

WHERWELL TO HURSTBOURNE TARRANT

'Quiet, sleepy little village as Wherwell looks today, in the time of the Saxon kings and till the destruction of the Abbey it was a place of no small importance.'

D.H. Moutray Read, 1908

This is a stretch of the Test Way which strikes deep into some of the most remote country in Hampshire. It continues along the Test valley via Wherwell and Longparish and then departs from the main river along the Bourne, a tributary that passes through St Mary Bourne from its source near Hurstbourne Tarrant.

Wherwell (pronounced Wer-rell) was once renowned for its abbey, which lay alongside the present Victorian church, close the site of a manor house called Wherwell Priory. Founded in 986 by Queen Elfrida, widow of King Edgar, it was one of three Benedictine nunneries of royal foundation in Hampshire, the others being Romsey Abbey and Nunnaminster, Winchester (see pp. 22 & 108).

During the rebuilding of the church in 1856–58 several relics of the ancient building were found, some of which can be seen at the west end of the church. These include the remnants of a Saxon cross that was reworked as a corbel in the 13th century.

The whiff of scandal which surrounds the lives of Edgar and Elfrida has made Wherwell Abbey a subject of perpetual interest. The story is told in an inscription on a tall stone cross which stands in Deadman's Plack Copse two miles north-east of the village, just off the A303 Basingstoke–Andover road.

Erected in 1835 by Colonel Iremonger, who owned Wherwell Priory, the monument tells how Elfrida's first husband, Ethelwold, was slain in the forest by King Edgar, who wanted her for his second wife. It seems that Ethelwold had been sent to bring back Elfrida for the King but instead courted her himself! Elfrida is said to have connived at Ethelwold's murder. Moreover, it is alleged that at Corfe Castle she killed King Edward, Edgar's eldest son by his first wife, with her own hands so that her teenage son Ethelred could succeed to the throne.

That is the legend: in fact, scholars believe that Elfrida had no hand in Edward's death, which was carried out by members of Ethelred's household to get rid of a king whose violence and intemperance were threatening the realm. Nonetheless, Ethelred's succession was shocking and a few years after the death of Edward, Elfrida took the veil and came to Wherwell to found the abbey, possibly as an act of penitence.

Footbridge to Wherwell

The abbey acted as a school for young girls and also as a convenient place for ladies to be sent for a 'rest cure' by their noble husbands during periods of disenchantment: both Cnut and Edward the Confessor made use of this facility.

Amongst the abbey's substantial endowments was City Mill, Winchester, which has been preserved, albeit in a later form. After the surrender of the abbey in 1539, some at least of the 24 nuns then in residence probably continued to live together under the abbess, Morphita Kyngsmill.

After the dissolution the abbey buildings were completely destroyed and the only memory of the nunnery to survive until recent times was the making of Easter 'cakes' in the village. In fact, these were thin wafers stamped with a seal said to be that of the abbey. The wafering tongs and special recipe needed were passed from mother to daughter.

The Test Way continues along a steep track leading to New Barn and **Harewood Forest**. Just before the path enters the forest there is a superb view to the east, marked by a water tower in the shape of an inverted cone six miles away at South Wonston, north of Winchester.

Down to the right through the trees is the white disc antenna of the Science and Engineering Research Council radio telescope and space station at Chilbolton. This stands on a former airfield, set up in September 1940 and used by American and British fighters until after the end of the war. Spitfires, designed in Southampton by R.J. Mitchell, were also assembled and tested here by Vickers-Armstrong.

Beyond this point the path runs through Harewood Forest, once the hunting grounds of Saxon kings and still the haunt of deer. The woodlands that exist now are a remnant of Chute Forest, a huge tract that once extended to Savernake in Wiltshire and covered much of the high downs of north-west Hampshire. The water table must then have been much higher and many of the 'dry valleys' ran with water.

WHERWELL TO HURSTBOURNE TARRANT

When in the early 1600s the poet Michael Drayton wrote of Hampshire in the 'travel poem' *Polyolbion*, he referred to 'the sprightly Test arising up in Chute'.

The Test Way continues to **Longparish** via Gavelacre, a small hamlet above Bransbury Common, a famous fishing beat of the river. Harry Plunket Greene in *Where the Bright Waters Meet*, a minor classic published in 1924, calls the common 'one of the most romantic spots in the South of England'. It was here that he witnessed a remarkable event, the visit of a cuckoo to a reed-bunting's nest. Bransbury Common, he says, 'belongs by prescriptive right to the snipe and the duck and man is an outrage on the landscape'.

One who would have shared his enthusiasm for the wildfowl, though with different intentions, was Colonel Peter Hawker of Longparish. His *Diary*, first edited and published in 1893, tells of the enormous carnage that he carried out in this part of Hampshire, and on the South Coast.

Although the Test Way does not extend to the northern end of the Longparish, where the Hawker family home stands, no account of the village is complete without Colonel Peter, who fought with Wellington and spent much of his retirement chasing game after sustaining a bullet wound during the Peninsular War.

The church at Longparish, which is reached across the lovely green below Middleton House, contains many memorials to the Hawker family. There is also a touching tribute to John Buffin, a 'faithful servant' whose remains were placed, as he had requested, next to those of his former mistress. This memorial was presumably placed here by the colonel, who is also commemorated, on a simple plaque placed in the church by his second wife Helen. She was a constant companion on his shooting exploits, often trudging miles in bitter weather.

The colonel was also a fisherman and took as many fish from the Test as he could catch. But he was no purist — he often trolled for trout with a minnow, almost a capital offence in some quarters!

The first section of the Test Way after Longparish runs across an old gravel terrace which overlies the chalk. At one point the path crosses the former track of the Hurstbourne–Fullerton railway (see p.45), where the cutting clearly shows the river gravel. Set in the midst of woodland, with young trees growing in its bottom, the cutting is well on its way to becoming as mysterious as an ancient earthwork!

Most of this part of the path runs along the top of a valley which skirts the edge of Harewood Forest. On one side is mixed deciduous woodland, with the occasional stand of beech and patches of yew, the climax vegetation of the chalk. On the other is lovely folded downland with little dry valleys and acres of luscious grassland. There are deer, squirrels, pheasants and a wealth of smaller birds.

After crossing the B3400 road that runs between Andover and Hurstbourne Priors, the path crosses a tongue of land in the latter parish and enters the parish of St Mary Bourne. It then crosses the Harrow Way — one of the great prehistoric roads — which runs parallel to the Basingstoke–Andover railway, a branch from the London–Southampton railway built in 1854, fourteen years after the main line.

WHERWELL TO HURSTBOURNE TARRANT

Some of the excitement of rail travel in the early days comes from this entry in Peter Hawker's *Diary*, dated 21st October 1838: 'Up for a candlelight breakfast. Went up for the first time on the new railway: did 38 miles in an hour and thirty-one minutes: in town soon after twelve.'

One of the most dramatic parts of the Test Way is above **St Mary Bourne**. After passing Derrydown on the right, the path suddenly comes out on a shoulder of the Bourne valley with the village spread beneath. Immediately below is the Bourne Valley pub and a restaurant, The Bright Waters, called after Plunket Greene's book.

In the bottom of the valley at some times of the year is the silver ribbon of the Bourne Rivulet, an intermittent tributary of the Test, which dries up at the end of each summer and is reborn each spring. During the winter the rains are soaked up by the underlying chalk until it can take no more and springs then break out along the course of the stream.

Downstream can be seen a huge nine-arch viaduct at Hurstbourne Priors, which carries the railway line to Andover. In front, screened by a belt of conifers, is a large area of watercress beds, where advanced methods of mechanisation have been developed. Owned by Hampshire Watercress Ltd, the produce from the beds is marketed throughout the country as 'Vitacress'.

St Mary Bourne, locally known as plain 'Bourne', nestles below, a picture of placid, settled rural life. In front of it stands a large lake, created a few years ago by the local GP. Though only a few miles from the Test, the scene is quite different from anything found along the larger river.

The path descends to the main road where it meets the Portway, the Roman road that ran between Old Sarum (see p. 70) and Silchester in the north. Opposite the junction is a large house which takes its name from the old road and was once the home of Kathleen Innes, whose book *Life in a Hampshire Village* is mainly about St Mary Bourne.

Better known, however, is probably Joseph Stevens, who was the village doctor for many years in the middle of the last century. His *Parochial History of St Mary Bourne*, published in 1888, was reckoned to be a model of its kind.

When Stevens lived in this remote village there were still people who could remember old customs which had been completely lost elsewhere. It was fortunate, for a historian, that St Mary Bourne was, as one rector put it, 'half a century behind'. (Not so today: the church, for example, was one of the first to use recorded organ music.)

May Day was celebrated by local lads — Stevens calls them 'a band of half-washed chimney sweeps' — blowing horns made from twisted willow bark and dancing round a bower enclosing a young maiden.

More characteristic was the Bourne Revel, a sort of fair-cum-carnival which had as its highlight a jousting competition with sticks. This was held on a platform over the river near the square or 'summerhaugh'. The aim of the game was to draw blood from one's opponent. The clouts sustained were so severe that at least one St Mary Bourne man suffered brain damage and had to spend his last years in the county lunatic asylum at Fareham.

And the prize? Often it was as little as a 'gold-laced hat'.

Walking down into St Mary Bourne

Joseph Stevens, as might be expected of a doctor, did not approve of these 'sports', saying that they were the haunt of 'gipsies, vagabonds and ''gamesters'''. The latter were men who made a point of going round to similar contests held at Hurstbourne Priors and elsewhere.

Towards the end of his life Dr Stevens moved to Reading where he indulged a life's interest in antiquities as the honorary curator of the local museum. In his obituary in *The Times* there is mention of his efforts to rid the village of 'fever': this was smallpox, which had been rife in the district in the early part of the century.

Those who caught the disease were sent off to a remote cottage on the edge of the down near Doily Wood: those fortunate enough to recover often spoke of the good times they had whilst there! Kathleen Innes records that one curious belief current amongst cottagers was that nailing up a hot-cross bun each year and allowing it to fester would ward off the scourge of smallpox.

She also says that Dr Stevens was not adverse to simplifying his lot if sport called. Then he would leave the surgery in the hands of his housekeeper, with just two kinds of medicine — 'starters' and 'stoppers'. Medicine was, of course, still very primitive at this time and people often sought the help of bonesetters or 'gentlewomen' skilled in herbal remedies. And dentistry was in the hands of the local blacksmith.

Despite everything, it was said locally that folk from St Mary Bourne could 'live as long as they like'. Certainly Dr Stevens lived long (albeit in Reading), dying in 1899 at the age of 81. He is buried in St Mary Bourne, behind the church, beneath the yew tree that stands beside a

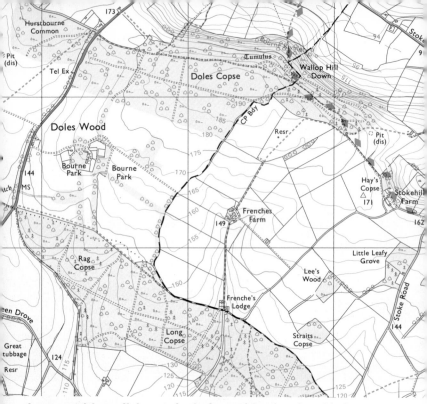

fragment of the wall that marks the limit of the churchyard before its extension in 1901.

The church is on the east side of the street. It has a very solid, substantial, square, castellated, flint-built tower. Amongst its treasures is the largest of the eight Tournai fonts known in the country, one of which has only recently been discovered, at Ipswich. Dating from the second half of the 13th century, four of them are in Hampshire, one in Winchester Cathedral. They are made from a black marble found beside the river Scheldt in Belgium.

The St Mary Bourne font used to stand on a sandstone base, but in 1927 this was replaced by one in Tournai stone. Not without difficulty: the first blank was broken and the second was cut to the wrong size and had to be reworked.

Most of the village is strung out along the course of the Bourne and straggles on to Swampton and Stoke. The Test Way turns left in the summerhaugh, opposite the George Inn (a stronghold of real ale), runs alongside the modern lake already mentioned and then cuts across the contours towards Stokehill Farm.

To the west is Doles Wood, the haunt of George Dewar, the naturalist and writer, whose best known book is probably *Wild Life in the Hampshire Highlands*. The remoteness and romance suggested by this superb title will be with us for the rest of this long-distance walk.

The Dewar family came to Hampshire in 1782 when Dewar's forebear and namesake, a tea planter from the West Indies, bought the manor of Hurstbourne Tarrant. After the first family home of the Dewars, at

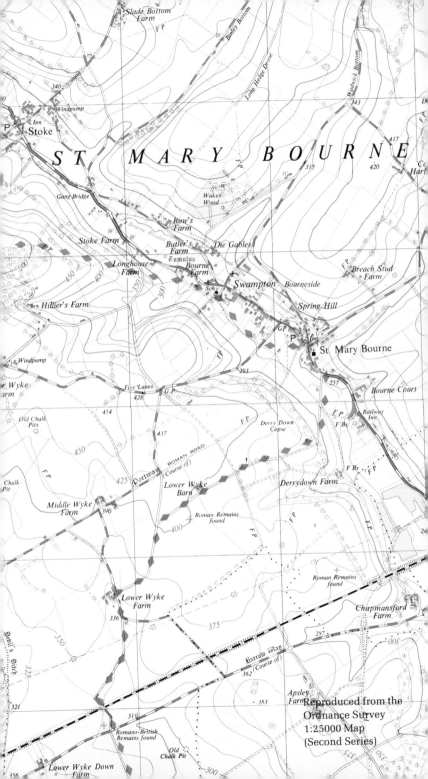

Enham, burnt down, they built Doles House, set in the wood which gave it its name, a fragment of the forest of Chute. It was 'built in the centre of dense and secluded woodlands miles from a town, almost miles from a village'.

George Dewar roamed these woods with his older brother and rode far and wide across the nearby downs. He became especially interested in bird life in the tradition of Gilbert White and W.H. Hudson and described many of his observations in *Wild Life*. It is easy to imagine peering with him into brambles for warblers' nests or sharing that rare — if not unique — finding, a baby cuckoo in a wren's nest.

During the First World War, Dewar was first a special constable at Buckingham Palace and later a war correspondent attached to the staff of General Haig. He was editor of two national periodicals, *The Saturday Review* and *The Nineteenth Century* and the author of twenty books, notably *Life and Sport in Hampshire* and *This Realm, This England*.

Beyond Stokehill Farm the path climbs on into the Hampshire Highlands which can be see in the distance, perhaps 7 – 8 miles away. It enters the copses of Wallop Hill Down, which falls away steeply to the right, and shortly drops down towards Hurstbourne Tarrant. The village is seen suddenly, nestling in a bowl with its prominent church steeple and the thin ribbon of the Bourne winding in the valley bottom. It is a picture-book view of an English village.

HURSTBOURNE TARRANT
TO
INKPEN BEACON

Woods near Linkenholt

HURSTBOURNE TARRANT TO INKPEN BEACON

'The village of Uphusband, the legal name of which is Hurstbourne Tarrant, is . . . a great favourite with me, not the less so certainly on account of the excellent free-quarter that it affords.

William Cobbett, 1822

Few churches reveal as much about their village as St Peter's at **Hurstbourne Tarrant**, though the clues are admittedly rather obscure.

Just inside the lych-gate on the left is what must be the largest gravestone ever laid. It commemorates Joseph Blount, farmer, who is said to have left instructions that his stone should be large enough for children to play marbles on it.

Blount was clearly an eccentric and perhaps this is why he became a close friend of William Cobbett the radical reformer and political journalist, who stayed at his home at Hurstbourne Tarrant. Part of Cobbett's classic book, *Rural Rides*, was written at Blount's home, Rookery Farmhouse, which still stands on the road to Andover, close to the village cross-roads.

Cobbett seems to have been obsessed by the naming of the two Hurstbournes, preferring Uphusband for Hurstbourne Tarrant and Downhusband for its sister village below. The 'husband' part of the name was, presumably, a dialect form of 'Hurstbourne'. In fact, the proper names relate to the former owners of the manors: Hurstbourne Priors belonged to the Old Minster, Winchester, and Hurstbourne Tarrant was granted to a community of Cistercian nuns at Tarrant Crawford, Dorset.

Today the only trace of the connection between the Hampshire and Dorset villages is the similarity of two wall paintings in the churches. That at Hurstbourne is on the north wall, and as Pevsner and Lloyd say, is 'unrestored and hence enjoyable'. It depicts the legendary tale of the three kings who were reminded of their mortality when they met three skeletons in the forest, hence the title, 'Three Quick and the Three Dead'.

Nearby is a slate tablet to the memory of artist Anna Lea Merritt (1844–1930), whose house The Limes stood alongside Rookery Farm. Born in Philadelphia, the daughter of a cotton manufacturer, she lived and worked for many years in Chelsea, before coming to Hampshire in 1891, following the death of her husband, art critic Henry Merritt. She exhibited a steady stream of pictures at the Royal Academy between 1878 and 1917, including the now unfashionable *Love Locked Out*, bought by the Tate Gallery, and a portrait of the novelist Henry James.

One of the people who sat for her was C. Kegan Paul, a partner in the firm which later published the book she wrote about Hurstbourne Tarrant, *A Hamlet in Old Hampshire*. It is a vigorous account of her sudden

The granary Parsonage Farm, Hurstbourne Tarrant

switch from Cheyne Walk to one of the most backward villages in the South of England. But the move suited her so well that she spent the rest of her days in Hurstbourne Tarrant. She wrote: 'Strange happiness and peace grew up in this rustic abode . . . When I settled down in these quiet fields, that feverish town-bred impatience was still in my veins: but luckily I could not gratify it. My first invaluable lesson was to wait.'

The American artist could never fathom the social class divisions of the English countryside and pinned her faith on the labourers, who seemed to be 'more sympathetic than their masters'. She admired the stoicism of men who said little, worked hard and had often ended their useful life by the age forty, after which they worked out their time breaking flints for road-mending.

One of Anna Lea Merritt's passions was gardening, and she may have shared her enthusiasm with another local resident, the amateur horticulturist Sir Arthur Hort. There is a memorial to him in the church, at the east end of the north wall, according to which he was a master at Harrow School for 33 years. Scholarship was in the family: his father was a distinguished Cambridge don who worked on the revision of the New Testament in the 1870s. In retirement at Hurstbourne Tarrant, Sir Arthur wrote two books on gardening, *The Unconventional Garden* (1928) and *Garden Variety* (1935).

Netherton

Earthworks

136

Manor
Farm

Pit
(dis)

Pit
(dis)

183

Pit
(dis)

171

Pit
(dis)

Heaven
Hill

Earthworks

Pit
(dis)

197

Resr

Pit
(dis)

Rymer's
Barn

Yews

FACCOMBE

166

190

195

Yews

Yews

131

Faccombe W

171

Yew

Grim's Ditch

Netherton Hanging Copse

Netherton Bottom

Faccombe W

Wilster
Copse

Pit
(dis)

Sawyers
Wood

121

Pit
(dis)

Pit
(dis)

Enclosure

Clinchorn
Farm

Day's
Copse

168

119

147

158

Pits
(dis)

114

Upton

150

140

145

135

The
Warren

Soper's
Farm

112

Ford

125

153

Ambley
Farm

River Swift

120

115

Fairway

Ambley
Wood

Ford

109

Upton
Valley

127

Spring
Row

Ppg
Sta

HURSTBOURNE TARRANT CP

Ibthorpe

Pit
(dis)

MS

210

200

102

101

Pol
Ho

Locke's Drove

148

POR

Hurstbo
Tarra

Locke's
Barn

PH

Windmill Lane

Dolomans Lane

120

Windmill Hill
Down

Windmills Farm

Windmills

160

140

175

Stoke

Windmill
Hill

Hurstbourne
Hill

A 343

B 3048

Lower

188

Beyond the church the Test Way continues along the side of the huge thatched barn of Parsonage Farm, which also has a fine timber-framed granary on saddlestones. The path passes behind the houses of the main street of the village and crosses the A343 Newbury–Andover road. A short diversion to the left, past the George and Dragon Inn and across the Bourne, leads to Rookery Farmhouse on the right, Cobbett's 'free-quarter', and above it Hill House, which stands on the site of Ann Lea Merritt's cottage and still has her studio in the garden.

Long before the American artist came to Hurstbourne Tarrant, Cobbett and his farmer friend argued and supped next door: there are more than twenty references to 'Uphusband' in *Rural Rides*. The book opens in 1822 with Cobbett leaving Kensington for the village, not by a direct route, which he reckons would take eight hours, but over the course of several days, via Guildford, Godalming, Odiham and Winchester!

It was only two years after the disastrous year in which the farmer-cum-political-journalist had been declared bankrupt and had had to sell his house and estate at Botley, near Southampton. His talk of 'free-quarter' was probably heart-felt, though Tony Brode in his *Hampshire Village Book* has suggested that he may have been referring to a practice of his host, Joseph Blount, who placed plates of bread and bacon on the garden wall of Rookery Farmhouse for the labouring poor. During the depression that followed the Napoleonic Wars, labourers' wages fell to very low levels — to six shillings, Cobbett records.

Guidebooks talk of the wall of the farmhouse containing a stone inscribed with 'W.C. 1825' and laid by Cobbett's own hands, but neither I nor the house's owner could find it: perhaps it should be restored.

The house next door, occupied much later by Anna Lea Merritt, seems to have been more than a simple thatched cottage. The front door was flanked by exotic and totally non-functional columns, which suggests that it may have had an 'arty' tradition even before the artist moved in. Sadly, it was almost totally destroyed more than 40 years ago in the sort of thatch fire that the artist wrote of in *A Hamlet in Old Hampshire*.

Long before the demise of her own cottage, a chance spark from a threshing machine set fire to a cottage in the village: the fire spread until a dozen houses had been destroyed overnight. Three days later the fire broke out again, with lesser consequences, but it led to talk of arson and a night-long watch was kept for several weeks.

Anna Lea's own cottage was threatened, though it escaped damage, but what later impressed her most was that there no mention of the blaze in *The Times*. She thought it very strange that there was 'foreign news in large type, and not a word of the ruin of a Hampshire hamlet.'

Until recently the tradition of art in Hurstbourne Tarrant was carried on at the Bladon Gallery, a centre for artists and craftsmen set up in the years after the last war. It was the idea of Doris Bladon-Hawton, a dog-loving eccentric, who made use of a redundant chapel that stands a short distance along the Newbury road. The gallery continued after her death but was recently closed and the premises sold.

The Test Way continues across the A343 towards **Ibthorpe**, alongside the dwindling stream of the Bourne. The water is incredibly clear in these upper reaches and flows over a grassy bed, dotted in spring with the white blooms of crowfoot. We are near the ultimate source of the rivulet, though in wet seasons the water continues in two branches — towards Henbarn at Upton, and Cockpit, in the Netherton valley. Hence the local saying:

When the Cock and Hen meet
Corn will be dear and hay cheap

The height of the water table used to be an important factor in the local economy and early in the year people would enquire anxiously: 'Is the water out?'

The path continues past Ibthorpe Manor Farm, with its fine Georgian farmhouse and then takes to an old drove road to Linkenholt. But before leaving this delightful hamlet, it is worth looking out for Ibthorpe House, also Georgian, and renowned for being the home of Mary and Martha Lloyd, close friends of the novelist Jane Austen. Instead of turning along the drove road, the walker should continue a short distance to a junction with the Upton Road, where the house stands to the right, in its own grounds.

Jane Austen often came to see the Lloyds from Steventon, about 15 miles to the east, where her father was rector. The families first became acquainted when the Rev. Lloyd became rector at Deane, which adjoins Steventon. After his death in 1789, the Lloyds stayed on at Deane for three years and then moved to Ibthorpe to make way for Jane's brother James and his wife Anna.

Both the Lloyd sisters, who lived at Ibthorpe with their mother, were later to marry into the Austen family, Mary to James, after the early death of Anna, and Martha to Francis (later Sir Francis), who became Admiral of the Fleet. Although Mary was welcomed into the family with enthusiasm, and is described as 'sensible and good-humoured', it seems that her tendency to dominate James and to complain endlessly of 'poverty' irked Jane.

Returning to the Test Way, the path beyond Ibthorpe continues along a track of packed chalk and flint, no doubt like all country roads on the downs before the advent of tarmac. The drove is well marked with solid hedges of oak, dotted with holly and yew.

To the left are superb views of the rolling downs of the upper Bourne valley, a mosaic of woodland, ploughland and pasture, divided by old boundaries and stretching as far as Conholt. Hereabouts much of the land is sheep country, bleak open downland, in sharp contrast to the sheltered lushness of the meadows of the lower Test valley, where the walk began.

The path soon runs roughly parallel with a large strip of woodland, Faccombe Wood, which was once much more extensive and merged to the south with Doily Wood, which ran on to the outskirts of Hurstbourne Tarrant.

Further on, overhead power lines cut across a right-angled bend in the path: about 300 paces beyond the second cut is Grim's Ditch, an ancient earthwork now overgrown with oak, hawthorn, elder and wild cherry. Alias Wodensdyke, it forms the boundary between the parishes of Linkenholt and Hurstbourne Tarrant, and is said to have been a Saxon boundary.

Former school and church, Linkenholt

The path leads to **Linkenholt**, a tiny remote upland community that is more like an overgrown farmyard than a village. In this part of Hampshire, living has never been easy and in the past 70 years the population of Linkenholt has halved. At Netherton, a mile to the east, is the site of a church and village which have been deserted in recent times.

The church at Linkenholt dates from 1871 and contains several relics from an earlier structure, notably the Norman doorway. Alongside is the tiny schoolhouse, built to match at about the same time. Both church and school have window arches decorated with Shepherd's Crowns, presumably taken from the local chalk.

The former school, which is now used as an office by Linkenholt Manor Estate, is a delightful brick and flint building reminiscent of a New England settlement. No bigger than a bungalow, with a tiny bell tower, it was built to house 40 pupils and continued in use until 1938.

The Test Way continues through the grounds of the present manor house, a huge dwelling with 42 rooms, built in 1907 with a ballroom added in 1935. It is said to have one of the earliest forms of double-glazing.

Beyond Linkenholt the path strikes across a field towards a prominent 'yellow brick road'. This forms a convenient landmark and guide for the next stretch of the walk. In the distance is a typical North Hampshire scene: small dry valleys with patches of woodland, like lichen on a rock.

The 'yellow brick road' winds its way along a valley bottom between the wooded slopes of Hart Hill Down and Linkenholt Hanging (not Hanger) on the left and Combe Wood. It is a welcome change after the bleak downs: here it is cosy, warm and sheltered. Bracken, brambles and honeysuckle intertwine beneath a canopy of oak and silver birch.

View down from Inkpen

Climbing up Sheepless Hill

Halfway along the valley the path crosses from Hampshire into Berkshire (though only since 1895, when the boundary was changed and Combe left Hampshire). But within a few hundred yards, where the valley opens out, it changes county again, into Wiltshire. The route, which has so far been taking the line of least resistance, now turns right and strikes steeply up along the top of **Sheepless Hill**, Wiltshire, alongside oak woodland that is in Berkshire. The main arm of the valley we have been following continues up to the hamlet of Buttermere.

We are now well above the spring line in dry country watered only by dew ponds. In a memorable phrase in her book *A Hamlet in Old Hampshire*, Anna Lea Merritt talks of the disappearance of the Bourne in the summer, when she 'shrinks silently back to her cave under Sheepless Hill.'

The path cuts up across the contours with lovely views of folded downland behind, towards Tidcombe and Fosbury. It is a patchwork of soft light browns and greens — of chalk earth, deciduous woodland and scattered patches of conifers.

Ahead the horizon has become quite clear, a sign that we are climbing to the heights of the downs. The Test Way continues to the top of the valley that runs beneath Sheepless Hill; at its head the path takes a slight S-bend and crosses once more into Berkshire. To the west, about ten miles away, can be seen the hills which overlook the Vale of Pewsey. The route now follows an old drove road to a dew pond, Wigmoreash Pond.

Shortly, and with dramatic suddenness, the final stage of the walk can be seen — along a chalk escarpment, past **Inkpen Beacon** and Combe Gibbet to Walbury Hill. After a distance of nearly 50 miles the path has topped the watershed and reached one of the finest viewpoints in the South of England. The land falls 300 feet to Inkpen and the Kennet Valley below.

It is a place to stand with a map and a pair of field glasses on a clear day. It is also an ideal spot for hang-gliding and the members of the Thames Valley club, who have made special arrangements with local landowners, are often to be seen in flight.

Walbury Hill, where there are obvious remains of a hillfort, is the highest point in Hampshire, 300 feet above Old Winchester Hill and 100 feet higher than Beacon Hill. It is part of the same chain of high lands that runs from Wiltshire along the Hampshire–Berkshire borders and divides, further east, into the North and South Downs.

Geologically speaking, Inkpen Beacon is on the Upper Chalk and the escarpment, which is cut into lower layers of chalk, leads below to a plain on the Upper Greensand. Further north the plain continues on the eroded 'edges' of tilted chalk strata.

North of Inkpen Beacon are the most westerly limits of the tertiary deposits of the London Basin, which were laid down in the great chalk downfold that extends along the length of the Thames Valley to the East Coast. To the south is a fine view over the Hampshire and Wiltshire Downs and beyond. It is said that on a fine day the spire of Salisbury Cathedral can be seen.

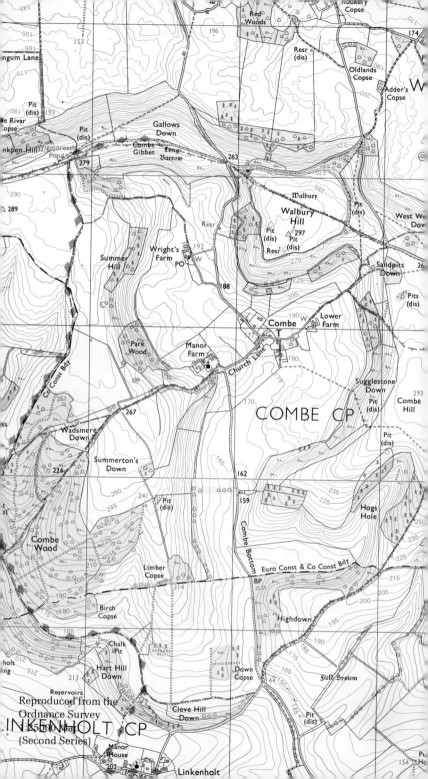

The rich plain spread out below leads in the distance to the Lambourn Downs. In the centre of the view is a tall thin mast which stands beside the Membury Service Station on the M4. This gives a fixed point with which to explore the scene: to the west is Newbury and straight ahead is Hungerford. Although it is not easy to pick out individual towns and villages (a topograph would be useful!), what is clear, however, is that there is a great contrast between the bleak downs and the lush plain below. In his *Wild Life in the Hampshire Highlands*, George Dewar made the same point, when he wrote: 'Compared with the unfruitful downs through which I had come lately, and upon which I could still look by turning round and moving a few steps, the country embraced in this view was as one great garden where all things had been carefully tended and watered.'

Dewar had climbed up from Combe to watch the sun set on a quiet evening in June that followed a windy day. What struck him was that the 'feel of June' was everywhere below, but up here there was little sign of the normal vigour of summer.

This realisation of the harshness of this upland country is perhaps a stimulus to leave the fine views and descend once more to the lowlands in which most of us live, to dawdle in the once-Hampshire village of Combe, to explore the little church of St Swithun's — granted for many years to King's College, Cambridge — and to return to the heartlands of Hampshire.

The ideal route might be by way of the Wayfarers Walk, a long-distance footpath that starts at Inkpen Beacon and runs 70 miles to Emsworth on the South Coast.

THE CLARENDON WAY
SALISBURY

Salisbury Cathedral

SALISBURY

*'Five rivers meet at Salisbury
— Avon, Wylye, Ebble, Nadder and
Bourne — and it was the rivers that
brought Salisbury down from the
hill, that gave it life.'*

Brian Vesey-Fitzgerald, 1950

The Clarendon Way runs across high land via long-forgotten rideway routes, through old forests that echo with the creaking of Roman waggons and the cries of kings and their kingsmen in pursuit of deer.

The walk stretches for thirty miles between two of the most celebrated cathedral cities in England. Winchester is much older than Salisbury, though the Wiltshire city sits in an area that has been a centre of religious activity for thousands of years. Ten miles to the north is Stonehenge, still an object of passionate interest at the Summer Solstice and the site of a temple since about 1800 BC.

The origins of Salisbury, however, lie two miles north of the city at **Old Sarum**, once quite separate but now touching the outer limits of suburbia. Here are the impressive earthworks of an Iron Age fort and a later Roman station. Old Sarum was also occupied by the Saxons, though Wilton was the capital centre during this period: hence, 'Wiltunscir', which became 'Wiltshire'.

The Normans also built a castle on the hill, the ruins of which are still there. William the Conqueror disbanded his army at Old Sarum four years after the Conquest and in 1086 called a council of all great land-owners to swear an oath of allegiance. And a few years later, following a policy of centralising power in the cities, a new cathedral was built within the ramparts, to serve a new diocese that united the rural dioceses of Sherborne and Ramsbury.

It was an ill-advised decision that led to trouble. The site at Old Sarum had no water and was exposed to the winds that tear across Salisbury Plain, which were not only unhealthy but often added an unwelcome accompaniment to the singing within the cathedral.

Moreover, the clerics had only been given a quarter of the site within the fort and were less than keen to share their devotions with soldiering men, or to remain in the castle's 'line of fire'.

The life of the cathedral community itself, worshipping in the building completed by St Osmund in 1092, was however a cause for celebration. St Osmund, who had been Chancellor of England, took pains to set up at Old Sarum a constitution which became a model of good ecclesiastical administration and one that is largely followed to this day. Unlike Winchester, which was run by monks, the Wiltshire cathedral was controlled by a chapter of secular canons with three principal 'executives' beneath a dean: the chancellor or secretary, the treasurer and the precentor, who looked after the choir and music.

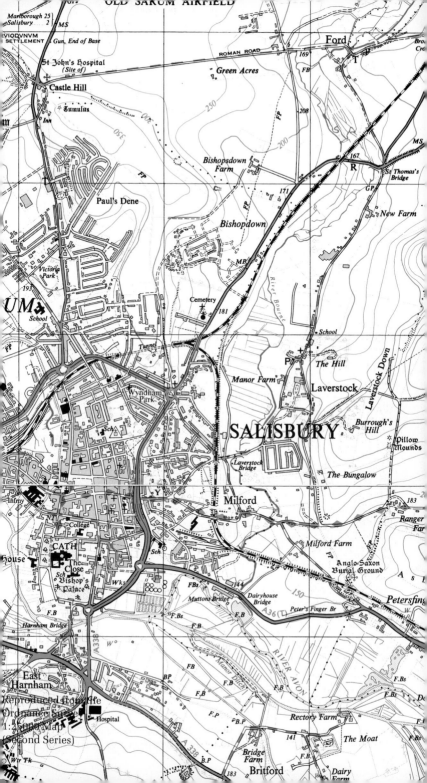

SALISBURY

The Old Sarum site was not given up easily. St Osmund's original church, 173 feet in length, was extended to almost twice its size in the 12th century: (the lines of the walls have been determined and marked out on the turf). Even then, the canons must have been unhappy with their site — the rationale for which was essentially that of the self-contained Iron Age fort (see p. 34). It did not allow for the trading opportunities being opened up in the middle ages to towns with accessible market places.

The decision to move must have been a painful one, and it was not until 1217 that Bishop Richard Poore, newly appointed after 19 years as dean, sought and obtained the permission of the Pope. His first thought was to build at Wilton, where there was an abbey of Saxon foundation, but the abbess — no doubt keen to retain her local monopoly — refused and so he chose a riverside site in his own diocese, about two miles to the south, in the parish of St Martin's. Once the decision to build the new cathedral had been made, the whole of the old city started to move to the new site.

At least, that's the popular view. But, as historians have pointed out (most recently John Chandler in his refreshing new look at Salisbury's history, *Endless Street*), the transition was undoubtedly longwinded and complicated. The unsuitability of the Old Sarum site to trading (cf. Romsey Abbey and its town, p. 22) probably meant that the lay members of the city, many of whom lived outside the fortified walls, drifted away before the new site had been chosen. This trend may have forced the canons to abandon the status quo and make a fresh start.

The low-lying site they chose, amply watered by the Avon and its tributaries, was part of the common fields of the bishop's manor of Myrifield. New **Salisbury** was laid out on a grand scale, with generous provision for a large market place and an extensive cathedral close. Gradually people moved to the new city, and the old site became almost deserted. A survey of 1377 showed only 10 people living at Old Sarum, compared with more than 3000 in the new city.

The 'false start' of the Normans brought one great advantage to the new city, for it meant that the **cathedral** was built with all the elegance of Early English design. It became what many people regard as the most beautiful cathedral in the country, though others think it rather 'cold'.

The most prominent feature is, of course, the steeple, which soars 404 feet into the air, but this masterful landmark was in fact an afterthought, added more than a hundred years after the start of the building in 1220. The original design was for a stubby tower, which was later heightened in two stages and topped with the steeple in 1330.

The steeple itself was built around a wooden scaffold which is still in place, together with a windlass that was used to draw up building materials — and is still used.

The name of the bold mason who masterminded this feat, which added 6,400 tons to the central tower, is unknown. But his skill and the faith of the canons who approved the scheme gave the city the medieval equivalent of Nelson's Monument or the Telecom Tower.

It also brought some problems, which continue even today. Despite the addition of extra stone vaulting below the tower and additional but-

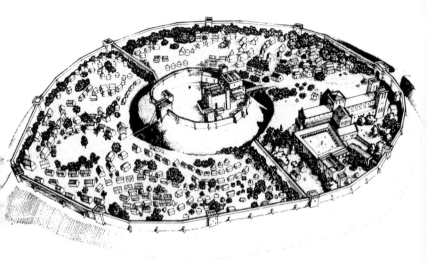

Reconstruction of Old Sarum

tressing within the clerestory wall, the pillars of the supporting walls at the crossing of the nave started to bend. The effects can still be seen.

By the 15th century inverted double arches were added above the main arches of the choir transepts and stone girder arches were built to tie-in the piers on which the tower and steeple rested.

Overall direction of the building of the new cathedral, which is the only medieval cathedral to be built in one period, was in the hands of one of the canons, Elias de Dereham (who also directed the building of Winchester Great Hall, begun two years later, see p. 115). The mason for the earlier work was Nicholas of Ely.

The elaborately carved west front, the cloisters (the largest of any in an English cathedral) and the fine octagonal chapter house — where the business of the cathedral is enacted — were all the work of another man, known as Richard the Mason.

The Trinity Chapel at the east end of the cathedral was the first part of the building to be completed, in 1225, and shortly thereafter the move from Old Sarum was symbolically demonstrated by transferring and reburying the bodies of St Osmund and two other former bishops. The elaborate shrine which was erected over St Osmund's grave was later moved and can now be seen on the south side of the nave, west of the south transept. Until the reformation brought pilgrimage as a whole into disrepute, this shrine was a common object of travellers to Salisbury, particularly after 1457, when St Osmund was canonised.

The famous bishop is still celebrated each year on the day of his death, 4th December, when a procession to the south-west side of the Trinity Chapel, the original site of his reinterrment, takes place at evensong.

SALISBURY

In the few years that Bishop Poore served the new cathedral — he was appointed to the see of Durham in 1228 — Salisbury began to achieve a tremendous reputation for scholarship and the roots of a 'university' akin to Oxford and Cambridge started to grow up in the city. There are now a number of schools at Salisbury, and a theological college, but its early claim to be a major centre of learning was not maintained.

The cathedral library does, however, have some extremely rare and valuable manuscripts from this period, including the finest of the existing copies of the Magna Carta. Apart from a five-year sojourn in a quarry during the last war, this famous declaration has been at Salisbury continuously since 1225, a decade after it had been agreed at Runnymede.

Other manuscripts, many of them beautifully decorated, include 70 dating from St Osmund's foundation, the Sarum Psalter of the 10th century and the Sarum Breviary of 1440. Even older than any of these is a single page of the Old Testament in Latin, which dates from the 8th century.

There is also a collection of early scientific treatises donated by Seth Ward — a friend of Sir Christopher Wren — who became bishop of Salisbury in 1667, a few years after the incorporation of the Royal Society, of which he was a founder member.

The library is situated above the east side of the cloister and is reached by a winding staircase that ascends from the south-west corner of the south transept.

Among the other treasures of the cathedral is a very early clock, said to be the oldest in England. It dates from 1386 and was originally installed in a detached bell tower, which was removed in a late 18th century restoration by the much-criticised architect James Wyatt. The clock stands at the west end of the north aisle.

For walkers who can spare an hour or two, there are many other memorials and artefacts which help to tell the story of the city and illustrate the first part of the Clarendon Way.

The overall shape of the cathedral is that of a double cross, with two sets of transepts, the smaller running from the choir. At the first crossing the outcome of adding the enormous weight of the spire to the fabric is apparent: there is a marked deflection in the slender Purbeck columns beneath the tower.

Structural repairs to counteract the weight of the tower and spire seem to be the legacy of each generation. Following the repair of iron ties and stonework in the 1950s, a canon wrote only a few years ago: 'The rest of the spire was carefully repaired at the same time, and it should now be secure for hundreds of years.' Alas, no! A new scheme has just been launched to raise the necessary funds to carry out yet another operation.

Whatever new work is done, let us hope that one of Salisbury's quirks is kept — namely, a dip in the spire of nearly 30 inches to the south-west, as first revealed in a survey carried out by Wren.

Near the cathedral is the Salisbury and South Wiltshire Museum, which contains amongst other things a large display on Stonehenge and a reconstruction of Old Sarum. Despite its drawbacks — especially the crampness of its quarters — the old city must have looked an immensely romantic stronghold to the canons and citizens who approached it from afar. No wonder they craved a cathedral with a spire that could be seen for miles!

To the south of the cathedral is the Cathedral School, a prep school for boys, including 16 choristers. It is housed in the former Bishop's Palace, one of the first houses to be erected on the new site in 1220.

The close itself is enclosed on two sides — the river completes the job — by walls which were built using the old stones of the Norman cathedral and other buildings from Old Sarum. Living there must be rather like being up at an Oxbridge college: the main gates start to close at 9 o'clock and late-night revellers must enter via the night porter.

The walls enclose a fine group of buildings, many of them dating from the first years of the cathedral. There is a particularly fine spread of buildings that face the west front and back onto the River Avon, including Wren Hall, the Wardrobe, Arundells, the North Canonry, the Old Deanery and the King's House, where Richard III and James I both stayed.

The bishop himself lives in the most secluded part of the close, in the South Canonry in the south-western corner.

There is much else to see in Salisbury besides the cathedral, including several fine timbered houses that belonged to the 'wool barons', men who bought the fleeces of the huge flocks that grazed on Salisbury Plain and turned them into cloth for export from Southampton. One such building is The Hall of John Halle (a very quarrelsome man), now used as a cinema and on the route of the Clarendon Way. It is reached by taking the High Street gate out of the close and turning right at W.H. Smith's into New Canal, which leads into Milford Street.

Although this road now only leads to a suburb of the city, it once was the main way to Winchester and was called after the Hampshire capital. Indeed, Salisbury in general is an interesting area to look at the effects of change on road patterns — not only the removal of the city from the Old Sarum site but also the influence of two other centres, the Saxon capital of Wilton and Clarendon, the site of a short-lived royal palace which lies on the path to the east.

Old Sarum was served by no less than five roads built by the Romans, including a through route between the Mendip lead mines at Charterhouse, near Cheddar, and Winchester. A Saxon road linked Wilton, Milford and Clarendon and continued through Pitton to meet the Roman road at Winterslow Common.

The main approach from the south was to Milton, via Stratford Tony, but all this was changed when in 1235 Harnham Bridge was built to the south of the close. This provided a route to Salisbury over the Avon and, as Leyland put it, 'was the totale cause of the ruins of Old-Saresbyri and Wiltoun'.

At the end of the medieval period the route to Winchester via Clarendon fell into disuse, possibly due to enclosure of the parkland around the palace or to the building of St Thomas's Bridge, which provided an alternative way to the Roman road via Laverstock. This is today a minor road, which turns off the Clarendon Way to the left between a Youth Hostel and Godolphin School.

SALISBURY

The Clarendon Way follows the former Saxon road to Clarendon. It leads across the Bourne at **Milford Bridge**, where the mill house still stands, and continues along a hollow way called Queen Manor Road. From here there is a fine view to the right, towards Petersfinger, where an extensive Anglo-Saxon burial ground was found beside the railway bridge.

Beyond is Longford Park, beside the Avon, and Clearbury Down, while to the right on a spur is Odstock Copse and Odstock Hospital, world famous for the pioneering work of its plastic surgeons, who developed techniques to repair the appalling injuries suffered in the last war by airmen.

Our path continues to the east, leaving behind the valley of the Avon, which runs to the sea at Christchurch via Downton, Fordingbridge and Ringwood. Rising in the Vale of Pewsey to the south-east of Devizes, this famous water is renowned for its fishing, but unlike the Test or Itchen it is fished mainly for its coarse fish, especially barbel.

The Avon was one of the first rivers to be canalised, following a 'publicity stunt' carried out by the water-poet John Taylor and others, who rowed a wherry from London to Salisbury via Christchurch. But the task proved to be much more difficult than envisaged, and though a canal of sorts was opened in 1684 it became disused within twenty years. Similarly, another attempt to link Salisbury to its markets, this time at Southampton, also failed (see p. 27).

The Clarendon Way now continues under Ashley Hill and then up a scarp slope to King Manor Hill. Behind is a view of the cathedral spire, which almost exactly bisects the valley we have been following. Yet even when the path reaches the top of the escarpment it is only level with the middle of the spire, which rises for a further two hundred feet.

Today this part of Wiltshire is totally rural, an area of open downland, copse and pheasant rearing. But for several hundred years the eyes of the traveller would have turned from the cathedral towards Clarendon Palace, an imposing royal residence that stood at the top of the hill.

CLARENDON PALACE
TO
BROUGHTON

Old track out of Salisbury on way out to Clarendon

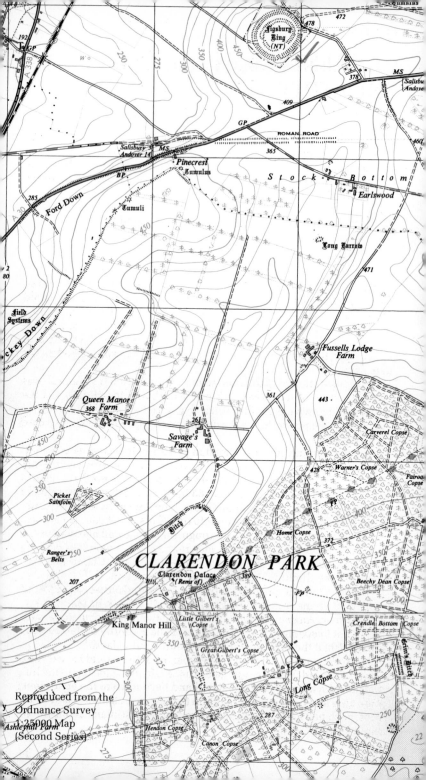

Figsbury Ring (NT)

478

472

192

GP

Wo

250

350

400

450

480

275

300

409

378

MS
Salisbu
Andove

GP

ROMAN ROAD

460

365

Salisbury
Andover 14

MS

Pinecrest

BP

Tumulus

Stock Bottom

Earlswood

285

Ford Down

A 30

Tumuli

450

Long Barrow

471

2
80

Field
Systems

ckey Down

Fussells Lodge
Farm

361

443

Queen Manor
Farm
368

261

Carverel Copse

450

Savage's
Farm

Warner's Copse

428

Fairoa
Copse

400

350

Picket
Sainfoin

FP

300

Home Copse

Birch

372

Ranger's
Belts
250

CLARENDON PARK

350

W

207

Clarendon Palace
(Rems of)

389

Beechy Dean Copse

300

FP

300

FP

FP

King Manor Hill

Little Gilbert's
Copse

350

Crendle Bottom Copse

Great Gilbert's Copse

225

300

Long Copse

250

Ashley Hill Farm

287

Hendon Copse

275

Canon Copse

300

22

CLARENDON PALACE TO BROUGHTON

'I used to walk out . . . with Mr and Mrs Lamb of an evening, to look at the Claude Lorraine skies over our heads melting from azure into purple and gold, and to gather mushrooms, that sprang up at our feet, to throw into our hashed mutton at supper.'

William Hazlitt on Winterslow, quoted by R.L. Brett, 1977

Clarendon Palace is one of the best-kept secrets of the Wiltshire countryside. It was a hunting lodge for Norman kings and played an even more important part in the life of the Plantagenets. Here in 1164 Henry II held a council of bishops and barons that had far-reaching implications for the relationship between church and Crown. It also led to the murder of Thomas à Becket, who attended the gathering.

The Constitution of Clarendon, which resulted from the council, was a reaffirmation of the power of kings over that of the church and the pope. It laid down clearly the crimes that were to be tried by the Crown and denied the protection of the church to clerics who had committed civil crimes.

The men who travelled to Clarendon to witness this great event would have seen a relatively modest building, but in the following years Henry II started to develop a huge palace on the site. On the northern edge of the escarpment he built a great hall, 83 by 51 ft, and dug a wine cellar in the chalk. Further extensive additions were made by his grandson, Henry III, who turned Clarendon into one of his finest country houses.

All that remains today is a single fragment of flint wall about 25 feet in length. It stands near the track that runs between woods stretching beyond King Manor Cottage, which is where the Clarendon Way emerges after climbing the scarp slope of Ashley Hill.

The constitutional importance of Clarendon is advertised on a plaque fixed to the remaining piece of wall by Sir Frederick Bathurst, a Victorian owner. An extract reads: 'The spirit awakened within these walls ceased not to operate till it had vindicated the authority of the laws and accomplished the Reformation of the Church of England.'

A traveller approaching the palace from Salisbury would have entered a large courtyard from the west gate. To the left, along the top of the hill, stretched the kitchens and great hall and beyond were the apartments of the king and his queen. In addition to their own chambers and wardrobes, each had a private chapel, served by Augustinian canons from a nearby priory.

CLARENDON PALACE TO BROUGHTON

The cathedral 'architect', Elias of Dereham, carried out much of the work for Henry III, including the building of a chapel beside the king's bedroom. It was an elaborately decorated building with gilded angels and images of saints on the walls and repeated rings of green and yellow tiles on the floor. Two other rooms in the king's apartments — the Antioch Chamber and the Chamber of Alexander — were richly decorated with wall paintings, depicting legendary stories and heroic events.

The queen's rooms were also decorated with wall paintings: in her hall stood a fireplace with marble columns and a mantle carved with the months of the year.

Although the court only came to Clarendon twice a year — in the summer and around Christmas — the evidence from excavations carried out before the last war suggest that some of the most skilled masons worked on the decorative stonework, as shown by a fine boy's head on display in Salisbury Museum.

In addition to the royal apartments and private chapels, the palace also had a large chapel and a range of offices, including an almonry, bakery, napery and chancellery.

After the death of Henry III, Clarendon was never again as important. It was last used by Henry VI in 1453 when he spent a year in the country during a bout of insanity. The Commonwealth sold it to raise money for soldiers' pay and later Charles II gave it to one of his courtiers, after which it passed through a number of hands, including those of Lord Chancellor Hyde, who was the 1st Earl of Clarendon. In 1737 a new mansion house, which still stands, was built about a mile to the south-east.

Beyond the palace the Clarendon Way runs for a short distance along a track and then, after a few hundred yards, slips into woodland on the left and continues amidst trees until it reaches Pitton.

The woods are mainly of oak with hazel, though there are occasional beeches and patches of conifer plantation. Here are the remnants of forests which once stood on all the heavier lands that stretch between Salisbury and Winchester, merging with those of the New Forest to the south. Indeed, until 1216 a single warden kept both Clarendon Forest (which included Melchet in Wiltshire and Buckholt in Hampshire, see p. 88) and the New Forest. This vast tract of woodland provided the ideal country in which Norman kings and their kinsmen could hunt and even today it is still inhabited by deer.

Pitton was one of a number of villages situated on the edge of Clarendon Forest — the others were Farley, East and West Grimstead and Alderbury — all of them ministered to by the priests from Ivychurch Priory, who also served at Clarendon. When the palace became disused all these places were for convenience lumped together in one parish, Alderbury. The existing parishes are therefore little more than a century old and until their inception the villages enjoyed considerable independence.

Ivychurch still appears on the map in the names of a copse and house to the north of Alderbury.

Pitton was the home for many years of Ralph Whitlock, author of more than 70 books, who now lives in Yeovil. In a recent article in *The Hatcher Review*, which records the history of Wiltshire, he has written

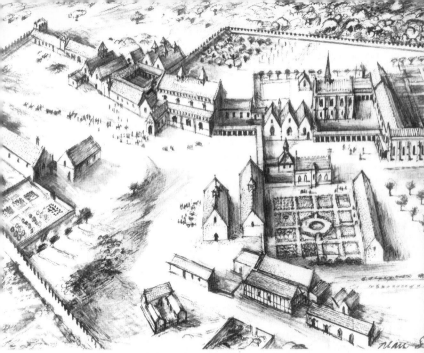

Reconstruction drawing of Clarendon palace

about the village, and in particular about what he calls 'a class of independent smallholder'. In the last century these men earned a living from a variety of casual jobs — hoeing, shearing, harvesting and also working on their own in the woods. In the autumn they would buy a block of standing woodland on the Clarendon Estate or elsewhere and work on it during the winter, making a variety of wooden articles such as hurdles, thatching spars, rakes and suchlike.

Perhaps as they worked, particularly with the hoe, they hummed that famous Wiltshire ditty which has the memorable chorus:

> The vly, the vly,
> The vly be on the turmut —
> 'Tis all me eye
> Fer I to try
> To keep fly off the turmut.

Mr Whitlock recalls: 'By the 1920s that way of life was becoming obsolete, but I remember seeing old men trudging along, rush baskets with protruding billhooks slung over their backs, on the way to their stand in Clarendon Woods.'

The Clarendon Way takes a remarkably straight path through the former forest before breaking out of the trees above Four Cottages on the outskirts of Pitton and passing on to the village.

Pitton clusters under an escarpment that is locally called Green Hill. It is now largely a dormitory for people who work elsewhere and the farming life that Ralph Whitlock has described in his book *A Family and a Village*, written as a series of letters to his grandson in California, has disappeared.

81

CLARENDON PALACE TO BROUGHTON

In the 1920s the farming lands around Pitton were divided between about a dozen small farms that grew cereals and had a few cows, chickens and pigs. Traditionally — like so much of Wiltshire and Hampshire — this had been sheep and corn country, until the agricultural depressions of the late 1870s bankrupted those farmers who had not managed to change their practices.

Pitton used to have a winterbourne — an intermittent stream. The path crosses its dry bed just before the village crossroads. Records show that the water used to come up about once in seven years, but extraction of water for domestic purposes has lowered the water table so much that the stream has not appeared for many years.

No special provision was made for the 'flood' until the middle of the last century. The water was allowed to pour into the village and gather in great ponds, which became stagnant and foul as the flow declined. Following the death of three little girls from scarlet fever, villagers made efforts to clear a channel to allow the water to flow away.

'It was not completely adequate, though, allowing the formation of pools large enough for us boys to enjoy voyages on rafts made from barn doors,' says Mr Whitlock.

Pitton has long been a 'chapel' village, partly because for many years — until the division of Alderbury parish in 1874, mentioned above — it did not have a resident parson. The Methodist chapel, which stands a short way along the south-east arm of the crossroads, dates from 1888 and was built on a site which has had a chapel since 1830. Before the First World War, services would be preceded by an open-air roadside recital given by the village brass band.

There has, however, been an established church in the village since at least the end of the 12th century. It stands beside the Clarendon Way beyond the crossroads and is a small flint-built structure with a tower surmounted by a weathervane in the shape of a cockerel. This was made by a local blacksmith, Moses Webb, and dates from 1801.

The church was 'restored' in 1878, when the north aisle was built and galleries removed, no doubt once occupied by the village musicians that Thomas Hardy depicts so lovingly. Shortly afterwards the east window was donated by the owner of the Clarendon Estate, Sir Frederick Bathurst, in memory of his daughter.

The window with its distinctive 'nobbly-leaf background' was designed by Eamer Kempe and is said to be a fine example of his art. Below the crucifixion is a pelican wounding herself to draw blood for her youngsters, a symbol of the sacrifice of Jesus.

A small brass on the north wall of the chancel records the death in 1580 of Edward Zouche, a native of Ashby-de-la-Zouche. His family succeeded to Pitton after the dissolution of the priory of Ivychurch.

The area later became the property of Sir Stephen Fox, born nearby at Farley, who had a distinguished career managing the royal household, holding such posts as 'clerk of the king's kitchen', before making his name at the treasury. But he did not forget his native village, obtaining the services of Sir Christopher Wren's master mason to build a new church and Farley Hospital, an almshouse for the needy.

Pitton remained in the hands of members of the Fox family, later styl-

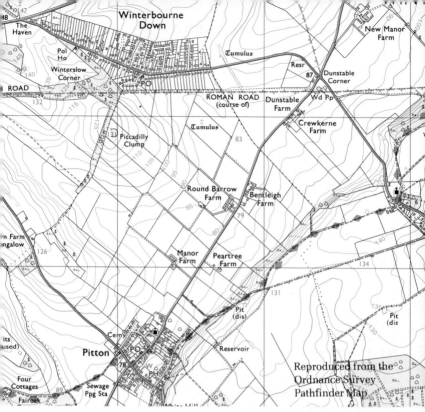

ed Earls of Ilchester, until 1912 when both it and Farley were sold. Many tenant farmers in the area acquired their land at this time.

The path passes out of the village, mounts the escarpment of Green Hill and comes out on open downland with fine views all round. On lower ground to the north-west is the modern village of Winterbourne Down, which lies hard against the line of the former Roman road. The scarp slope here was too steep even for the Roman engineers, who built terraces to take the road (see p. 86).

To the north is Porton Down, once a notorious centre for research into microbiological warfare and now an establishment which uses similar scientific methods for medical research and other peaceful purposes.

In prehistoric times the chalklands to the north were an important area for mining flints. At Easton Down, on the far side of the A30, an extensive system of U-shaped mine shafts dating from the Neolithic and Early Bronze Age ages has been exavated.

The sharp geological change that occurs hereabouts is well demonstrated by the great areas of woodland that can be seen to the south, on the heavier lands of the Hampshire Basin.

The path comes out at All Saints Church, **West Winterslow**, a flint-built structure with a square castellated tower. As at Pitton, when this church was restored one of the items removed was the gallery where, it is recorded, 'Psalmsody of the most unsavoury character was performed by rustics whose knowledge of singing was the very smallest'.

CLARENDON PALACE TO BROUGHTON

Winterslow consists of several separate settlements and has been dubbed a 'bits and pieces' village. The path passes behind the church to a stile and continues via a right-hand fork to Middleton and Middle Winterslow, which is best known for its association with the essayist and great man of letters, William Hazlitt.

Here he found his first wife, Sarah Stoddart, not by all accounts an attractive lady but one with the convenience of a house and a small income. She was the daughter of a naval officer, who had retired to Winterslow. She and Hazlitt lived in the village for several years.

The writer's career was not going well. He dabbled with literature and painting and had friendships with talented people, including Coleridge, Wordsworth and Charles and Mary Lamb, who were close friends of Sarah and had introduced the couple. But Hazlitt had problems with women. Coleridge criticised him for treating them as 'objects of sexual indulgence' and on one occasion he was literally chased out of the Lakes by men who objected to him harrassing their daughters.

Hazlitt's fortunes changed for the better after a few years at Winterslow with Sarah, when he obtained a post as a parliamentary and theatre critic on a London paper, the *Morning Chronicle*. The life of the journalist, with its insistence on deadlines, seemed to suit him admirably and he spent the rest of his life writing for several papers, including *The Times*. Hereafter, much of his life was spent in London, but he came back to Winterslow when he wanted to recharge his batteries and get down to some extended work.

He apparently treated his wife abominably, and in 1819 after his endless love affairs and financial crises, she left him. Even so, Hazlitt continued to seek the peace of Winterslow, staying at the Hut (now the Pheasant Inn) on the main Winchester–Salisbury road. The great four-poster bed he slept in was until recently still there. He once wrote: 'The *incognito* of an inn is one of its striking privileges'.

His witty prose contains many lines that must have been penned with the Wiltshire–Hampshire borders in mind, not all of it complimentary. Perhaps he had come across too many 'Private — Keep Out' notices when he wrote: 'There is nothing good to be had in the country, or, if there is, they will not let you have it.'

Of especial interest to the walker is Hazlitt's *On Going A Journey*. He loved travelling, which he described as 'one of the pleasantest things in the world'. He was also an enthusiastic walker and wrote: 'Give me the clear blue sky above my head, and the green turf beneath my feet, a winding road before me, and a three hours' march to dinner — and then to thinking! It is hard if I cannot start some game on these lone heaths.'

Hazlitt died at the relatively early age of 52 and confessed on his death-bed that it had been 'a happy life'. There is little doubt that the long periods at Winterslow were one of his delights, but for the village it is a quirky connection: for most people life revolved around earning a living and, in this dry downland, obtaining enough water.

The water problem was finally solved in 1935 when a local Water Society engaged a water diviner and decided to deepen a local well and pipe supplies to houses. A good supply was obtained at a depth of more than three hundred feet.

Cottage at West Winterslow

Earning a living at Winterslow has always been hard but would have been even harder without the activities of a pioneering local institution, the Winterslow Land Court. Set up in 1892 by a local landowner, Major Robert Poore, it provided a means for protecting the land rights of smallholders, who received 1999-year leases on plots from a quarter of an acre to 16 acres. The court, which attracted national attention, predated the Parish Council Act by three years.

Two years after the inauguration of the land court Major Poore and others set up another scheme for improving the lot of local folk, the Winterslow Weaving Industry, later amalgamated with the Stonehenge Woollen Industry. It was a cottage-scale business which turned local fleeces into hand-woven cloth of a very high craft quality.

The strangest job in Winterslow was, however, that of truffle hunting, carried out by the men of the Collins family for 250 years or more. This special skill was handed from father to son and can be tracked back to a pack of trained poodles, which were brought to the village from Spain in about 1700.

The last truffle-hunter in Winterslow — and probably in the country — was Albert Collins, who died in 1953. His father, Eli, was a well-known local character, famed for his velvet coat, who worked his dogs until he was 83. A special spike was used to unearth the precious fungus once it had been sniffed out by the dogs. Truffles were apparently particularly abundant on the Longford Estate beside the River Avon, home of the Duke of Radnor, who gave the Collinses free access.

The largest truffle ever found in the area weighed more than a pound and was discovered by Eli Collins in the presence of the Duke of Clarence, the grandson of Queen Victoria, who is said to have accepted it on her behalf.

Beyond Middle Winterslow the Clarendon Way follows the course of the Roman road for some distance, keeping to it when the modern road turns south towards The Common. It passes into a small recreation field called The Shripple, 'presented by Brigadier and Mrs Fisher of Hill Farm, Winterslow, in 1970', and then crosses a field to the left, passing under power lines and coming out in Red Lane.

A detour that can be taken here is to continue across the Shripple (crossing into the field halfway across) and take a path along the back of houses to a T-junction. Opposite stands a former school house and a church. The church, which is held by St John's College, Oxford, was built first, in 1860, and is remarkably plain and simple. The school, which followed nearly twenty-years later, is now used as a scout hut.

The Clarendon Way is rejoined at Red Lane by turning left and mounting Gunville Hill.

Keeping to the former Roman road, the path continues along Easton Common Hill towards Noads Copse. It follows a track that dips towards the Wiltshire–Hampshire border and then rises towards Buckholt Farm. Perhaps this is the place to contemplate the skills of the Roman engineers who built a network of roads that has only been matched in recent times.

The Winchester–Old Sarum road was an early Roman road built to take traffic between state-owned lead mines in the Mendips and the Roman port of Clausentum, near Southampton. The western part of the

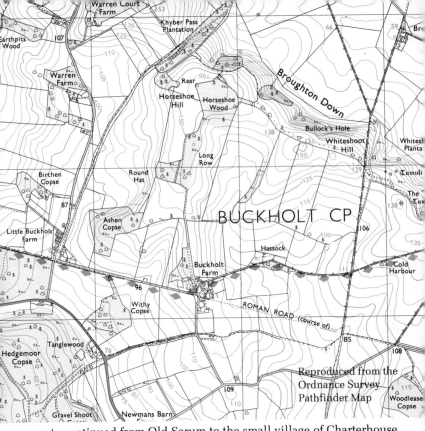

route continued from Old Sarum to the small village of Charterhouse, near Cheddar.

Roman roads were generally built by excavating a ditch or a series of holes and piling up material to form an embankment or agger. The surface of the carriageway itself, which was generally narrower, was then made up with local materials and often finished with gravel.

An excavated section of the Old Sarum road suggests that in this instance the gravel was probably laid on chalk. Also, the carriageway of the road was held together by side 'kerbs' of coarse gravel and chalk laid on a foundation of flints.

The line of the Roman road on the map tends to confirm the popular idea that the Romans always took a straight line between two points. In fact, although long sections were linear, the engineers provided zig-zags, terraces or cuttings to negotiate extremely steep gradients. There are several places where this was necessary on the Old Sarum road, which climbs over many north-south spurs between Salisbury and Winchester.

As already mentioned, terracing had to be used at Pitton to mount the steep escarpment to the north of the village. And at Hoplands, a few miles before the Sparsholt section of the road, the gradient was also eased, by zig-zag diversions.

The road has been studied in detail by archaeologist David Johnston and his students, who point out that lead was transported as large ingots

87

weighing about 150lbs. They were probably carried in groups of four by wagons drawn by a single ox, supplemented by extra animals at steep points. One of the ingots has been found, in 1783 at Bossington on the Test — but it raises as many questions as it answers.

Most intriguingly, the composition of the metal turns out to be similar to that of lead mined in Flintshire. Even so, archaeologists believe that the ingot probably came from the Mendips, though it could have been on its way to the Somerset mines for cupellation — the extraction of silver from lead.

Whatever the origin of the Bossington ingot, attempts to explain how it finished up in the river have included the suggestion that the final leg of the lead route to Clausentum was by barge down the Test. Mr Johnston and his colleagues point out, however, that if this were so the western stretch of the Old Sarum road would have been made for heavier traffic than its counterpart to the east — and this does not seem to be the case.

The Roman road beyond Winterslow would have cut through woodland, for deep forest then stretched virtually all the way to Winchester. Noads Copse and the similar patches of woodland in the area are remnants of Buckholt Forest, one of the hunting grounds of Saxon and Norman kings and their kinsmen. Further east lay Parnholt and West Bere, while to the north of the county were Pamber and Chute. William I, however, preferred more open woodland than that of Buckholt and the other forests and therefore turned his attention to the south, where he planted the New Forest. Gradually most of the older forests were cleared and cultivated.

After passing Buckholt Farm the path leaves the line of the Roman road and takes to a track leading to an old hollow way, lined with yews, which falls over the down to Broughton (pronounced Braw-ton). This was once part of the road between Winchester and Salisbury, but an understanding of the piecemeal way in which the direct Roman route was altered in later times must wait until another stage of the walk (see p. 94).

Between Buckholt Farm and the down the walker passes over one of the most recent additions to this part of Hampshire, a petrol pipeline that runs — unseen and unheard — from the Esso refinery at Fawley, near Southampton, to the Midlands.

BROUGHTON
TO
OLIVER'S BATTERY

Clarendon Way Country, near Broughton

BROUGHTON TO OLIVER'S BATTERY

'England was once dotted with 26,000 dovecotes, which were our forefathers' answer to factory-farming.'

Leaflet on the Broughton Dovecote

Broughton lies in the valley of the Wallop Brook, which rises five miles to the north and runs into the Test at Bossington, via Over Wallop, Middle Wallop and Nether Wallop.

The faintly ridiculous names of these beautiful villages come from the fact that they were once owned by the Wallop family, later enobled as the Earls of Portsmouth, who held estates in the north of Hampshire, at Farleigh Wallop, Hurstbourne Priors and elsewhere.

One puzzling feature of the Wallop Brook is the name Nine Mile Water, which is given to that stretch above Broughton. Some have suggested that it is a corruption of 'nine mills', but a simpler explanation is that, with due allowance for all twists and turns, the distance from source to confluence is in fact nine miles!

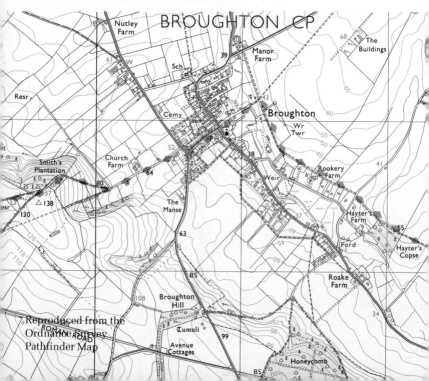

Reproduced from the Ordnance Survey Pathfinder Map

A well in the main street of the village dates from 1921, when a prolonged drought caused the Wallop Brook to run dry.

The Clarendon Way comes out in the centre of Broughton, opposite the church of St Mary's. It continues along a lane to the north of the church, past a prominent dovecote in the churchyard, one of only four similar structures in 'working order' in the country. One of these is at Old Basing House, near Basingstoke. Apparently, Broughtonians have always referred to it by its Latin name of *columbarium* — Columbidae is the biological name for doves and pigeons.

Pigeon meat was until relatively recently an important source of protein, particularly at the end of the winter, when vegetables and salted meat were scarce. The dovecote at Broughton has nearly 500 nesting boxes on the inside of its curved wall and provided about three and a half tons of fresh meat per annum. It was made part of the rector's endowment in 1341, though the present structure only dates from 1684.

Pigeons can be induced to keep laying eggs on a six-week cycle for seven years, with scarcely a break. The eggs were allowed to hatch and the young pigeons, called 'squabs', were reared until they reached a weight of about a pound. They were fed by the adult birds, who scoured the surrounding countryside for food, coming and going via a central turret at the top of the dovecote.

The gruesome task of slaughtering the squabs was carried out from a ladder fixed to a finely balanced rotating structure called a 'potence', a

clockmaker's word. The keeper would go from box to box by moving up and down the ladder and rotating it to new positions with a touch of the hand.

The key to the dovecote at Broughton can be obtained to view the potence, which was restored in 1984 to mark National Heritage Year.

The church itself is of Saxon foundation and was once held by the Archbishop of York. This unlikely connection was a legacy of its former position as a chapel attached to Mottisfont church, four miles to the south, which was founded in the 7th century by Wilfrid, Archbishop of York, during a period of exile in the south (see p. 27).

One interesting feature of the church is that the chancel does not run due east but 'nods' to the north to symbolise the fallen head of Jesus on the cross.

A memorial to a local doctor, Luther Owen Fox, erected at the west end of the church after his death in 1879, is of interest for its connection with an early experiment in what we would now call a collective farm. Dr Fox is honoured by 'old Queenwood friends', a reference to Queenwood College, a progressive boys' school set up a mile to the south of Broughton in 1847 in Harmony Hall. This grand building had been erected a few years earlier by Robert Owen and the members of the 'Home Colony of Associated Industry'.

This was an ambitious experiment in practical socialism which involved the lease of a thousand acres of poor chalky soil and ended in bankruptcy. One of the reasons for its failure was the lavishness of Harmony Hall itself, a three-storey mansion provided with the latest gadgets, including an advanced heating and ventilating system and a 'miniature railway' to carry dishes between the kitchen and dining room.

The set-up was absurb for an embryonic self-sufficient community, but for Owen, entrepreneur turned reformer, it was only the latest in a series of experiments to change the social order. His model industrial village, New Lanark, is now recognised as an extraordinary achievement. Even after the failure of Harmony Hall the Welsh idealist continued to advocate his ideas with passion in the hope that a 'new moral world' would come about.

Harmony Hall was destroyed by fire in 1903, but relics of the former community and college remain at Queenwood Farm.

Brought has an unusually early Baptist Church, dating from 1653. Intolerance of religious 'deviation' was, however, strong and the church's records are blank for more than a decade after the Restoration.

The Clarendon Way continues over the Wallop Brook and then takes a high path that runs parallel with the valley towards Bossington. There is a fine view of Broughton Hill to the right, across an area called Wallop Fields. Ahead is the white scar of the far side of the Test valley and down to the right lies **Bossington**, with its tiny church built in 1839 alongside Bossington House.

As the path approaches Bossington the small spire of the church at Houghton (pronounced Hoe-ton) can be seen about a mile to the north. This church is particularly interesting for several reasons and is worth a detour.

Churchyard and dovecote at Broughton

Here the growing atmosphere of religious dissent in the middle of the 17th century resulted in the forced replacement of one rector by another.

James Sessions, the man who lost his living, lived to see the end of the Commonwealth and was granted a memorial in Houghton church, which can still be seen at the north end of the altar rails. His successor, Thomas Warren, was less fortunate and in 1662 was turned out of his living for refusing to conform to the Act of Uniformity, after which he furthered his dissenting views in Romsey (see p. 24).

After Bossington the Clarendon Way takes to a public footbridge across one of the most celebrated trout streams in the world, the Test. Here it is a wide waterway, not as clean as further upstream, but nonetheless a fine river.

The path passes beside Black Lake Farm, where there are clear signs of the western bank of the 'Park Pale' that once enclosed a deer reserve. Then it crosses the course of the former Andover–Southampton railway, now used by the Test Way (p. 31).

The Test has always been a barrier for anyone travelling across Hampshire: it is deep and never runs dry. Various crossing points have been preferred at different periods. Perhaps the movement of the river itself has played some part (Bernard Aldrich, the Romsey water-keeper, says that the Ordnance Survey once recorded a shift of nearly 40 yards in 25 years!), but equally the 'best' route has varied with the fortunes of nearby communities.

The Romans chose the most direct line, crossing the river near Horsebridge, though the exact spot is not known. The Saxons may have allowed the route to the west to decay, using a road along the Wallop brook rather than the Roman road. However, according to C. Cochran in *The Lost Roads of Wessex*, the Normans revived the old road because it allowed easy access to the palace at Clarendon (see p. 79) and the forests en route.

During the 13th century, however, an alternative route via Stockbridge — one of the medieval new towns — gained prominence, and the preferred way from Winchester to the Test became the present line of the A272. To the west the medieval route passed through Broughton and rejoined the Roman road near Buckholt Farm.

The movement of the preferred route from the dense forests beloved by Norman kings to the open downland further north must have suited traders and travellers seeking the markets of Stockbridge and Salisbury, while many huntsmen had long forsaken the woodlands of mid-Hampshire for the more open glades of the New Forest.

Hunting and forestry had, however, for centuries been the main reason for the existence of such royal possessions as King's Somborne, which the Clarendon Way approaches after crossing the Test. Even now woodland crafts such as hurdling are practised here and there are strong memories of John of Gaunt's deer parks, which lay to the west and north of the village.

In fact, there is no evidence that this celebrated son of Edward III ever visited King's Somborne or hunted in its woods. But there seems little doubt that the equivalent of a wealthy man's 'recreation complex' was set up, complete with archery butts, the remains of which can still be seen to the south of the church.

The path climbs up out of the Test valley towards How Park Farm (echoes of one-time local landowner, William de Ow), beyond which can be seen traces of the eastern bank of the 'Park Pale', topped by a road leading to a tarmacadam works. The enclosure of deer parks was increasingly carried out during the middle ages as a means of enforcing the ruthless forest laws that William I and others introduced.

A licence to disempark John of Gaunt's deer park — i.e. to remove its special legal status — was granted in 1639: it was a signal, repeated elsewhere, to clear the woods for cultivation.

As the Clarendon Way approaches **King's Somborne** — locally called plain 'Somborne' — there is a fine view to the left, towards the higher lands of Marsh Court and Stockbridge. The village centre itself bears out the cliché that requires every English village to have the church, the pub and the school next to one another.

The school is particularly interesting since it was regarded as a model type of National School when it was built in 1842, apparently because it was 'large and well-organised'. Amongst those who came to see it and talk to its founder, the Rev. Richard Dawes, were Matthew Arnold, the prime minister Lord John Russell and Florence Nightingale.

Opposite the school is the Crown, a popular country pub. It has, of course, changed dramatically since the days when the walker could discover 'unknown' pubs in out-of-the-way places. This was still possible in the 1930s, when the author Gordon Lee stayed at a pub in King's Somborne that may have been the Crown. Here he met a local character called 'Mossie', who made a living from collecting and selling mosses and sprays of leaves for decoration.

In his book, *Beyond the Old Royal Road*, Lee describes the man's outfit: it would probably cause a bit of a stir in the Crown today. He wore a green jacket, knickerbockers, grey stockings, and had a red-and-white spotted hankerchief around his neck. A pheasant feather was stuck in his hat and he carried 'a hazel stick newly cut and trimmed'.

One interesting feature of Kings's Somborne is the war memorial in the village centre, which was designed by the distinguished architect Sir Edwin Lutyens, who is also responsible for the memorial at Stockbridge and the country house nearby, Marsh Court (see p. 33).

The route back to the Clarendon Way from the village centre passes alongside King's Somborne's river, an intermittent winter stream that never seems to have been named. It now rises in a field to the north-east of New Lease Farm, but has been known to start further up, to the north of the A272, where it has flowed over the road beside the Rack and Manger pub. Like the winterbourne at Pitton, it too has apparently been depleted by falls in the water table.

The path from King's Somborne climbs up out of the valley of the un-

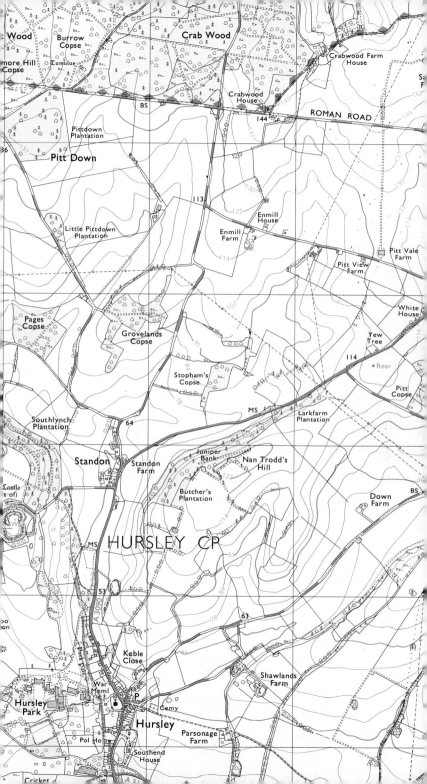

named river with fine views all round: back to the Test Valley, down to the village and to the south towards Parnholt Wood, another fragment of ancient forest. To the north is the hamlet of **Ashley**, though little of it can be seen from the path. It was once a place of some importance and a detour by footpath or road is worth while.

The Normans built a castle at Ashley, to the west of an earlier Roman site. Traces of the bailey earthwork remain, but little is known of the purpose of the castle, though it probably held a garrison to protect the route of the Roman road to the south. Evidence of domestic activity suggests that it had been abandoned by the early 15th century.

The tiny Norman church at Ashley, which has a chancel arch only four feet wide, stands within the former bailey and dates from the 12th century. Two large 'squints' added after the original building give the congregation a view of the altar.

The Clarendon Way can be rejoined from Ashley by continuing along the road to **Farley Mount**. The path is met below Ashley Down where it briefly touches the Roman road before cutting up to Beacon Hill, which was presumably used for signalling. A mile to the south stood Farley telegraph station, built in about 1831 on the 'new line' between Whitehall and Plymouth, which was never completed. This was intended to replace an earlier type of semaphore which was built in 1806 and ran to the south via Toot Hill.

Between Ashley and Beacon Hill the road passes a monument to four 'unknown' airmen (now identified), who died when a Junkers 88 aeroplane was shot down to King's Somborne after being pursued from Manchester by a Spitfire.

Returning to the Clarendon Way before the detour, the path continues along a field boundary above King's Somborne, keeping the buildings of Hoplands to the right. After passing through a patch of woodland it emerges on the route of the Roman road and follows it for a short distance before swinging away to the south and then briefly rejoining it beside Beacon Hill.

The Clarendon Way climbs to the top of a ridge on its way to Farley Mount, It is an area of classic chalk downland topped with yew, the climax vegetation. To the north are beautiful views with scarcely a building in sight.

Ahead is what could at first sight be mistaken for the steeple of a very small church: it is in fact a monument, and a monument to a horse! Two inscriptions — one high up and the other inside a shelter — tell the story behind this folly, thirty feet in height, which is a popular destination for people from Winchester.

Underneath lies the body of a horse that in 1733 apparently leapt into a chalk pit twenty-five feet deep 'with his master on his back' and lived to ride on. Indeed, in the following year he won the Hunter's Plate in the annual races held on Worthy Down, to the north of Winchester, when he was entered under the name 'Beware Chalkpit'.

The incident is featured in *Sporting Reminiscences of Hampshire* by 'Aesop', the pen-name of W.N. Heysham, who dedicated his book to a 19th century secretary of the Hampshire Hunt, William Graeme. Chalk pits were, it seems, one of the hazards of hunting and in 1847 a very

Farley Mount Monument

similar near-miss was survived by Mr Barton Wallop, who was out with the Hursley Hounds with Prince Edward of Saxe Weimer and others.

The Farley Mount memorial was restored in 1870 by Sir William Heathcote, a prominent Hampshire man and the owner of Hursley Park, two miles to the south-east of the monument.

There are fine views from Farley Mount, particularly to the south, but nothing much can be seen of Winchester to the west, which lies hidden in the valley of the River Itchen. In this landscape the famous cathedral city is situated between a cluster of tall radio masts on the western outskirts, which are clearly visible, and the distant mass of St Catherine's Hill, which shows to the right.

The Clarendon Way continues along the length of Farley Mount Country Park, which is owned by the Hampshire County Council and includes Crab Wood, two hundred acres of ancient coppice-with-standards woodland, managed with the Hampshire and Isle of Wight Naturalists Trust as a nature reserve. Together with the adjoining West Wood, owned by the Forestry Commission, the area forms an extensive remnant of the Forest of West Bere.

Farley Mount has all the ingredients of a superb country park: old woodland, open downland, bridleways, footpaths, car parks hidden amongst the trees and nature trails. It is a place to walk, walk the dog, play ball games and generally soak up some country air.

The Clarendon Way skirts the edge of the woods and runs mainly through great stands of beech, the home of squirrels. But much of the woodland is of oak with hazel 'stools', which are traditionally cut on a seven-year cycle to provide wood for hurdles, wooden rakes and other everyday country articles.

BROUGHTON TO OLIVER'S BATTERY

Early in the year, before the oak trees get their leaves, the floor of the wood is covered with flowering plants — the so-called pre-vernal species such as wood anemone, violet, and wild strawberry. The ground beneath beech trees, which cut out as much as eighty per cent of the light, is much less fruitful and the only plant which will grow there is dog's mercury.

In addition to oak, hazel and beech, Crab Wood contains wild cherry, birch, silver birch, crab apple, goat willow and field maple. It is the haunt of nightingales.

Adjacent to Crab Wood, in the midst of West Wood and about half a mile to the north of the former Roman road, is the site of **Sparsholt Roman villa**. This will shortly be opened, together with explanatory signs, as part of Farley Mount Country Park. It was excavated by arch-aeologist David Johnston in the late 1960s, when the Forestry Commission wanted to bulldoze an access ride through the area.

Apart from adding further details to an understanding of the Roman country estate in Hampshire, this particular dig produced a great surprise. After excavating part of the perimeter wall of the courtyard of the villa it was decided to dig a mound that was suspected, rightly, to be that of the dwelling house. When the original floor level of the villa was reached the archaeologists discovered a mosaic, which was complete with the exception of a small part on one side. Later it was lifted and is now on display at Winchester City Museum.

Several phases of building were uncovered during the dig. The mosaic was in the third building to be put up on the site, a house measuring 110 × 35 feet built in the late 3rd or early 4th century. The almost perfect preservation of the mosaic is probably due to the fact that the villa was allowed to decay naturally, although a later timbered hall was built near-by using plundered materials.

Even though Sparsholt villa was in a relatively remote country district, albeit close to a major town, its owners probably managed to live in some style. The first building on the site had a three-room bathroom suite and a later, aisled building had even more elaborate facilities. No doubt the occupants could indulge in the traditional routine: first stripping, then a spell in the warm room, followed by the *caldarium* — an intensely hot room where the body might be oiled and scraped clean. Then, to cool off, a return to the warm room before taking a final cold plunge.

Ideal treatment after a long walk! But fear not, the Clarendon Way is entering its final leg. The path now leaves the course of the Roman road, turning north after a crossroads at the edge of the country park. Alongside Crabwood Farmhouse, there is a particularly well preserved portion of the original ditch which ran along the length of the Roman road.

The Way passes a Home Office Radio Station and follows a lane to the top of Stanmore. It then turns south through one of Winchester's suburbs, Oliver's Battery.

WINCHESTER

Winchester High Street looking up towards the Castle site

WINCHESTER

'They used to come this way,
Buying candles and relics at the cheap jack stalls
Which brimmed over in the North Aisle,
As noisy a crowd of pilgrims
As ever wore out shoe leather on a short cut to Heaven.'

Patrick B. Mace, 1973

Winchester was at the centre of church and state affairs when England was made. It was here that Saxon, Norman and Plantagenet struggled to create the political unit that arguably has had more influence than any other single country on the direction of the civilised world in the last millennium.

Moreover, Winchester is a pleasurable city where steep hills and chalk streams provide a dramatic setting for a dramatic story. It stands in a gap between high chalklands to the east and west and on a river which leads by gentle gradients to Southampton, the largest town known in Saxon times, a major port and a vital link with the continent.

The first sight of the centre of the city from the Clarendon Way comes as the path leaves Oliver's Battery, just outside the boundary of the city: it was from here that Cromwell threatened the city and obtained its surrender.

In the centre of the view, and still the largest building in the city by a very long way, is the cathedral: at a distance it is not perhaps beautiful, but it is undoubtedly commanding.

Winchester College, the famous public school, lies to the south of the cathedral, where the square tower of its chapel can be seen rising amidst an extensive campus.

At the extreme left of the scene is a distinctive white tower belonging to Winchester Prison, a high security gaol. Alongside is the tall tower block of the headquarters of the Hampshire Police. To the right, marked by a prominent verdigris clock tower, are the main offices of the Hampshire County Council, and further round the steeples of Christ Church and St Thomas's.

To the right of the cathedral is the prominent green roof of the clock tower of the Victorian guildhall and the wooded slopes of St Giles's Hill. A map and a pair of field glasses will enable much more of this panoramic view to be picked out, and with it in mind the walker can now go down to look at the detail.

The path follows an old hollow way which runs down to the Southampton–London railway line, opened in 1840 and the first to be built in Hampshire. To the right are views of the Itchen valley and the southern outskirts of the city — on this side of the river is the square tower of the Hospital of St Cross and on the other side the rounded outline of St Catherine's Hill.

The Clarendon Way meets the St Cross Road, the main road between Winchester and Southampton and formerly the Roman road that ran to Clausentum, the Roman port situated on the Itchen, near Bitterne.

The Hospital of St Cross is the best known of several charitable homes and almshouses that still remain in the city. It was originally founded at the beginning of the 12th century by Bishop Henry de Blois for 'thirteen poor men, feeble and so reduced in strength that they can scarcely . . . support themselves without other aid.'

Later, in 1446, another bishop of Winchester, Cardinal Beaufort, gave the hospital a second endowment, the Noble Order of Poverty, intended to help men of good birth who had fallen on hard times. He also rebuilt the hospital, with the exception of the church, and added the fine gateway.

The brethren — as they are called — total twenty-four and can be distinguished by their dress: those with black gowns and the silver cross of Jerusalem belong to the older order, while those with a plum-coloured gown and a badge depicting a cardinal's hat and tassels are endowed by the Beaufort foundation.

Financial problems are still matters for controversy at St Cross: the Charity Commissioners have recently given the trustees powers to charge the brethren for such things as meals, heating and lighting. One of the longstanding traditions of St Cross which will be safeguarded, however, is the Wayfarer's Dole, a small glass of beer and a thin slice of bread given to anyone who asks.

Alongside the hospital runs the **Itchen**, a chalk stream that is famous in fishing circles for its trout. Although not perhaps so celebrated as the

103

Test, it is nearly so and has attracted many men whose names are legendary in the sport. G.E.M. Skues used to fish at Abbots Barton above Winchester, where he pioneered methods of catching trout with a type of wet fly called a nymph. But his methods, which are now widely followed, caused such a uproar amongst dry-fly purists that he was forced to fish elsewhere.

The Itchen is said to have been made navigable in the 13th century by Bishop Godfrey de Lucy, who supposedly raised the water levels by creating a lake in the upper reaches at Alresford, one of the medieval 'new towns'. The river was definitely canalised over much of its length at the end of the 17th century, albeit after much shilly-shallying. Barges could then be floated to Woodmill on the outskirts of Southampton and taken with the tides lower down to Northam.

A navigable river as far as Winchester would have been a definite asset in earlier times, since many of the major buildings of the city were built in stone, obtained mainly from quarries on the Isle of Wight. But when Winchester College was built in the late 14th century, for example, it seems that most of the stone had to be carted the ten miles from the estuary of the river to the city.

For many Wintonians the meadows of the Itchen are the city's 'common'. A few years ago Government plans were made to route the M3 London–Southampton motorway across these hallowed wetlands. But such uproar was created at public enquiries by otherwise sober citizens that plans were changed and this section of road — the last link in the motorway — will now probably be built on a line to the east of St Catherine's Hill.

'Hills', as it is known to Winchester College boys, has an almost mystical significance for most Wintonians. It is topped with a prominent earthworth which has been excavated and shown to be a fortified British site that was possibly taken by storm and destroyed c.100 BC, like other Iron Age forts elsewhere (see p. 37).

The hill is named after the chapel dedicated to St Catherine of Alexandria, which once stood there. Built in the 12th century, it was granted at the dissolution to Thomas Wriothesley, 1st Earl of Southampton, who demolished it.

The Clarendon Way continues along the river and at Garnier Road passes a building dating from 1878 which contains a sewage pumping set and an incinerator. It is perhaps typical of a cathedral city to name this essential but mundane facility after one of its deans, Thomas Garnier.

The path now runs through the meadows alongside that part of the city chosen in the late 14th century by William of Wykeham for the building of St Mary's College, the original foundation of **Winchester College**. At the time it stood just outside the city limits and was therefore built so that it could be defended against attack.

Wykeham wanted to set up a 'feeder' school for New College, Oxford, which he had founded a few years before. He was also prompted by the effects of the Black Death, which only twenty years before had carried off large numbers of young men who would otherwise have entered the administrative offices of the church.

Chamber gateway of Winchester College

Wykeham was not only Bishop of Winchester but was twice Chancellor of England. In the mould of churchmen of the day, he was a capable and powerful man of affairs: he founded Winchester College to provide the type of education that would fit young men for administration in the church and public service, and in so doing he is credited with the beginnings of the public school system.

When Henry VI later founded Eton he purposely modelled the new school on Wykeham's foundation and took great pains to make sure that the spirit of the place was transplanted. He therefore made the headmaster of Winchester the first headmaster of Eton, took over some of the scholars and even, in a mystical gesture, had several cart-loads of soil dug up from the precincts of the college and spread about the grounds of the new establishment at Windsor.

The Clarendon Way approaches the college between the playing grounds and the river. This is where on a summer's evening you are likely to see, on the right, a college boy fly fishing in his straw boater and on the left a game of cricket. Perhaps cricket above all else is the game that is played most passionately at Winchester: it was, after all, the school that produced Douglas Jardine, the England captain whose 'body-line' tactics won the Ashes but nearly destroyed sporting links with the Australians during the controversial tour of 1932–33.

The high spot of the sporting year at Winchester is the cricket match against Eton, first played in 1760 or earlier. In one memorable match of 1923 the batsman J.L. Guise made 278 for Winchester, and even then the match was lost!

WINCHESTER

Like Eton, Winchester has its own game, Winchester Football, a curious sort of contest played between parallel nets that in the 'hots' resembles a rugby scrum. Originally it was played with lines of junior boys 'kicking in' in place of the nets, apparently to prevent the ball from continually being lost down the slopes of St Catherine's Hill, where it was first played.

The path comes out at New Hall, a modern college building which was opened in 1961 and is often used for concerts and recitals. It turns right and then left into College Walk. Ahead is the official residence of the Bishop of Winchester. It is a surviving wing of a much larger house built after 1674. The Clarendon Way turns right at the house and circles round the outside of the old city wall, but those who want to see the college must turn left.

The earliest parts of the College are around Outer Gate and Outer Court leading to Chamber Court, which contains the chapel and dining hall and where scholars have their rooms. At the entrance to the treasury below the hall hangs the portrait of 'The Trusty Servant', a curious and rather unpleasant painting that often adorns college publications. It shows a man with a pig's head, ass's ears and stag's feet. The snout is padlocked shut so that 'no secrets he'll disclose' and there are a variety of tools in his left hand, including a shovel, a pitchfork and a broom.

An archway leads from Chamber Court to Old Cloister, where dons were once buried and there is the gravestone of a scholar who is said to have 'gone to heaven instead of Oxford'. Alongside, to the west, is School, a late 17th-century red-brick building, where a low-key type of speech day called 'medal-speaking' is held.

There is a good deal more to see at the college and visitors are encouraged to join one of the several guided tours that are made each day.

The final stretch of the Clarendon Way runs to the centre of Winchester, alongside the river and the city wall. To reach it from the College, double-back to the Bishop's house and take a signposted path.

To the left are the picturesque ruins of **Wolvesey Palace**, fortified in the mid-12th century by Bishop Henry de Blois, brother of King Stephen. It was one of several strongholds used by de Blois, including Merdon Castle, near Hursley.

Wolvesey was at the centre of the struggle for power that flared up between Stephen and his sister Matilda, following the death of their father, Henry II. Over a period of twenty years, Henry de Blois took first one side then the other, until eventually he settled for Stephen, whose forces took up positions at Wolvesey and waged war against Matilda and her forces in the Castle to the north-west. Much of the city which lay between the rival factions was destroyed, including the Norman palace.

The Clarendon Way meets the river in an area called The Weirs and continues alongside the river to Bridge Street, where it emerges opposite **City Mill**, a National Trust property which was once held by Wherwell Abbey. The present building dates from 1743 and is the only mill that has survived in Winchester, which once had a large number — for grinding corn, for fulling or bulking-out cloth and for 'tawing', a process for making leather supple.

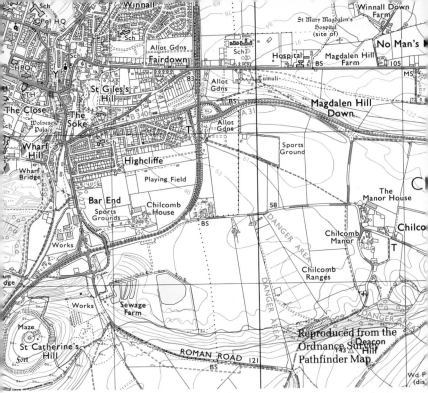

One of the assets of the Roman town, called *Venta Belgarum* — the town of the Belgae, a British tribe — was probably a mill for weaving woollen cloth, an industry which continued to be a cornerstone of Winchester's wealth during the middle ages.

Just before reaching the City Mill, near the almshouses of St Mary Magdalen, the Clarendon Way passes the only visible part of the Roman wall of the city, built of flint in the 3rd century AD. Excavation in several places has shown that the medieval wall was built on top of the Roman wall, which enclosed an area of about 144 acres.

The forum and market place of the Roman town lay to the north of the cathedral. Amongst the many finds unearthed in the city is an inscription with letters almost a foot in height. This is larger than any other Roman inscription found anywhere in England and suggests an enormous public building, probably dedicated to 'Antonius'.

One of the natural features of Winchester that makes its main street so dramatic is **St Giles's Hill**, the steep wooded down that rises at the east end. It was here that a huge and internationally important fair was held each year, originally for 16 days following the last day of August. Rights to the fair were held by the bishop, who literally took over the city, and the neighbouring town of Southampton, and also controlled all trade within a distance of 'seven leagues'.

The fair started with a ceremony at each of the city's gates, where the keys were handed to the bishop's officers by city officials, who also surrendered the 'tron', the machine used to weigh wool. Merchants came from all parts of England — and from the continent — to trade mainly in

107

woollen cloth, but also in a wide range of other goods. The hill was laid out as a virtually permanent 'exhibition area', with special shops and streets for each of the trades. And whilst the fair was in progress the whole city was dedicated to its cause, which each year made a fortune for the bishop and traders alike.

The fair was at its height in the 14th century but continued, in a much reduced form, until the last century. Today St Giles's Hill is a park and provides an ideal vantage point from which the main features of the centre of the city can be viewed. Immediately below is Bridge Street, and then the Broadway, which continues as the High Street to the Westgate at the top of the city. It is dominated at the entrance by the bronze statue of King Alfred, which was erected in 1901 to celebrate the 1000th anniversary of his death (although scholars have shown that he actually died in 899).

Archaeologists are still trying to piece together the details of the transition between Roman rule and Saxon settlement — the so-called Dark Ages — but enough has been discovered from excavations in Winchester and elsewhere to alter the standard explanation that the Romans 'pulled out', leaving the country to conquest by Saxons in the early 6th century. Evidence for the presence of Saxons as early as the 4th century has now been obtained and it even seems possible that they first came to Britain as mercenaries, following the collapse of Roman power.

One vitally important outcome for the city during the early Saxon period was that in about 660 the King of Wessex, Cenwalh, who had been converted to Christianity like his father Cynegils, chose to transfer the West Saxon bishopric to Winchester, where a church stood.

The Old Minster, as it came to be called, was drastically altered over the centuries, culminating in a complete reconstruction in the late 10th century. At this time the newly-appointed bishop, Ethelwold, ejected secular canons and replaced them by monks who were said to be literally waiting outside the church! It was the start of a monastic revival that led to the famous Winchester School of illuminated manuscripts.

To return to King Alfred, he succeeded in 871 to the kingdom of the West Saxons and spent the early years in a bitter struggle to confine the Vikings to the East Coast. During this period he acted as the overlord of the English, though his great-grandson Edgar (959–75) is regarded as the first King of All England. Alfred believed in the value of literature and scholarship: living in his palace near the Cathedral, and weakened by a lifelong illness — probably malaria — he and his assistants translated books from Latin into English to make them more accessible to a wider audience.

Following a period when the Saxon port of Southampton had been the centre of activity in Hampshire, Alfred restored urban life to Winchester and made it his capital. He laid out a new grid system of streets, much of which survives, and made Winchester a great centre of commerce, industry and learning.

Alfred also built two great new monasteries, both of which have long gone — Nunnaminster, which spread from the Broadway to Wolvesey Palace, and the New Minster, which lay between (and almost touched) the Old Minster and the present High Street.

Former Assembly Room of Winchester, in the St. John's House

The New Minster, where Alfred was eventually buried, was not completed until after his death. Later the whole community moved to a new site outside the east gate of the city, Hyde Abbey, and Alfred's remains went with them. In 1760, long after the abbey had been dissolved and destroyed, workmen digging in the Hyde area of the city came upon two lead coffins, thought to be those of Alfred and his son. They sold them for scrap metal: all that is left of this great king is the inscription stone which lay on his tomb, which is now in the City Museum.

To the north and south of Alfred's statue are the almshouses and other buildings of St John's, a hospital similar to that of St Cross (p 103), but of much older foundation: it may even date back to Saxon times. Amongst its most valuable possessions were shops on St Giles's Hill, the site of the medieval fair.

The Clarendon Way passes the Guildhall, built for the city council in the 1870s. The foundation stone was laid by the Liberal politician Lord Eversley, a champion of rights of way and commoners' rights, to whom many are indebted for saving such places as Wimbledon Common and Hampstead Heath. He later came to live near Winchester, at Abbot's Worthy.

The Clarendon Way is now approaching its end. It turns left down Colebrook Street, which leads to the Wessex Hotel on the right. Beyond is the cathedral, which is approached by a path that runs along the back of the hotel.

William Walker, the diver who saved Winchester Cathedral

Unlike Salisbury, which dates from one period (see p. 72), Winchester Cathedral demonstrates a variety of architectural styles. The north transept, which juts out towards the Wessex Hotel, is the least altered part of the original Norman building, which was constructed between 1079–93 by Bishop Walkelyn.

The consequences of the Norman invasion were, of course, immense in a city which had been the capital of England. Saxon landholders in the area were ousted by William I's followers, the Old Minster was demolished and the last Saxon bishop, Stigand, ended his days in prison. The monks of the New Minster, some of whom died on the battlefield at Hastings, were forced to cede part of their meagre land in the centre of the city — close to the present City Cross — to enable the royal palace to be extended.

Winchester Cathedral, which was at least four times the size of the Old Minster, was built to signify by its sheer size that the Normans intended to take full possession of their new prize. The early workmanship, however, is not of high quality.

The central tower, for example, fell down in 1107 and the existing tower is the one that was built in its place, an example of decorated Norman architecture with a good deal more finesse than the earlier work.

The windows between the north transept and the west end of the cathedral were inserted in the 14th century, when major changes were made to the fabric. First, the Norman west end, which had flanking towers, was pulled down and replaced by the existing work, a process which shortened the original building by forty feet. Then, after William of Wykeham had become bishop, the entire nave was refashioned, in some cases by paring down the Norman pillars and in others by 'grafting on' the present facing, all in the English Perpendicular style. The windows on the north side reveal the two phases: the two closest to the west end, which are more squat, date from the earlier period of remodelling.

Wykeham's achievement gave Winchester one of the finest naves in Europe, a splendour which is all the more surprising for the dourness of the exterior. He was honoured with a chantry — a private chapel — one of the many in the cathedral. It stands in the central section of the south aisle. Further east, at the south-western corner of the choir is the chantry of Bishop Edington, who carried out the first phase of the 14th century work.

Both transepts of the cathedral still show the original Romanesque style of the building: clean-cut rounded openings supported by solid plain pillars, a design of simplicity and immense power.

Leading off from east side of the south transept is the presbytery aisle, which is reached via the pilgrim gates, a fine example of wrought ironwork which is probably as old as the cathedral itself. It was here that travellers filed to see the shrine of the Saxon bishop St Swithun, who died in 862. He was originally buried outside the Old Minster but his remains were later brought inside and then removed to the present cathedral at its completion in 1093. During the middle ages St Swithun's shrine was visited by vast numbers of pilgrims, many of them making their way from Canterbury via the Pilgrims Way. Like tourists today, some of them bought metal badges which they displayed on their hats or clothing to signify their visit.

St Swithun's shrine was destroyed at the reformation, but the position of the grave at the back of the choir is still marked, by a modern canopy in brass and wrought iron.

The north aisle of the cathedral is particularly sought out by modern 'pilgrims' for the grave of Jane Austen, who spent her final days in Winchester in lodgings alongside the college. The simple black slab above her grave makes no mention of her writings. One fellow author who came and recorded his appreciation is Rudyard Kipling, who wrote:

Jane lies in Winchester, blessed be her shade!
Praise the Lord for making her, and her for all she made . . .

On the west wall of the cathedral is a memorial to the Royal Hampshire Regiment, whose story is told in a nearby museum housed in the regimental HQ at Serle's House, Southgate Street. The regiment also looks after a famous local gravestone, that of the grenadier Thomas Thetcher, who died in 1764: it stands to the west of the cathedral, beyond the war memorial, to the right of the paved path leading to Great Minster Street. The inscription, no doubt penned by a keen officer, still offers sound advise to the thirsty walker. It reads:

Here sleeps in peace a Hampshire Grenadier,
Who caught his death by drinking small cold beer;
Soldiers, be wise from his untimely fall,
And when ye're hot drink strong, or none at all.

Winchester Cathedral

The Cathedral Close extends to the south of the church, over the area formerly occupied by the cloisters of the monastery. On the eastern side of the garth are five remaining arches of the cloisters, with the deanery beyond.

In the southern part of the Cathedral Close, across the green in front of the east end can be seen the Long Gallery, a red-brick wing attached to the deanery and used to accommodate Charles II in his last years. With his mistress Nell Gwynne installed a few miles outside the city, at Avington House (the dean wouldn't have her in the close!), he stayed here at a time when Winchester expected to regain at least some of the royal glory which it had lost, for the King was planning a country palace that owed its inspiration to Versailles.

It was to be built to the south-west of the city, where William I had

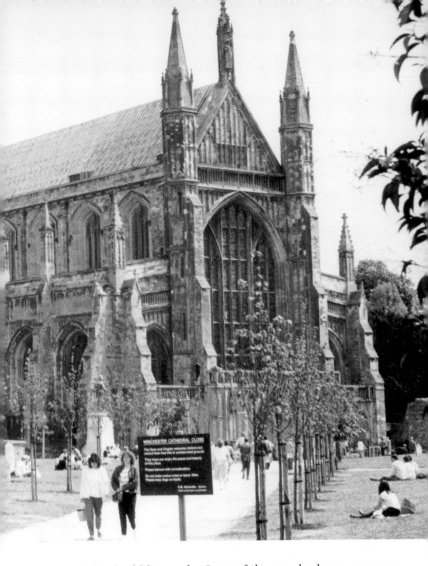

also decided to build his castle. Some of the grand scheme was completed before the king's death in 1685, but it never became the royal retreat it was planned to be and later served as a barracks. It was destroyed by fire in 1894, though the present barracks on the site reflect some of the grandeur of the original.

The castle site is reached by crossing back through the close and yard of the cathedral to the City Cross and then turning left and walking to the Westgate, a prominent fortified gatehouse at the top of the main street. The route passes the City Museum, which stands just outside the cathedral precinct. It contains a brass-rubbing centre and many interesting exhibits, including the Sparsholt mosaic (see p.100) and a model of the Old Minster.

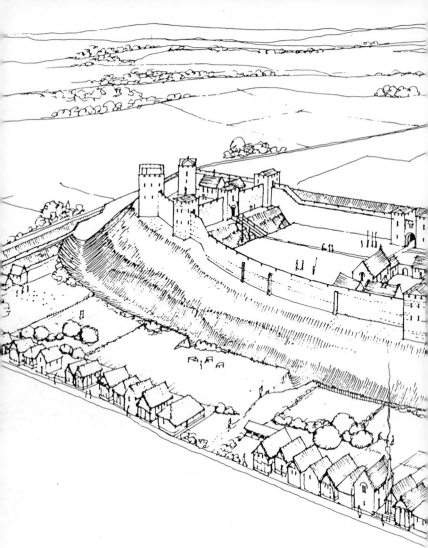

Artist's impression of Winchester Castle in the 13th Century

The **Westgate** is one of the ancient gates of the city, though the present building dates only from the time of Henry III and has 14th century additions. It is now used as a small museum and, in particular, contains a fine decorated wooden ceiling made for John White, warden of Winchester College. The work was carried out just before the marriage in Winchester of Mary and Philip, possibly in the hope (in vain, as it turned out) that they would visit Mr White's rooms after the ceremony.

The great Norman castle that once stood to the south of the Westgate was built in the year after the Battle of Hastings. Excavations carried out in 1967–69 show that William I cleared this quarter of the city and built over Saxon houses, many of which therefore await future archaeologists. It was here that the Royal Treasury was kept, together with the Domesday Book, which was compiled in Winchester.

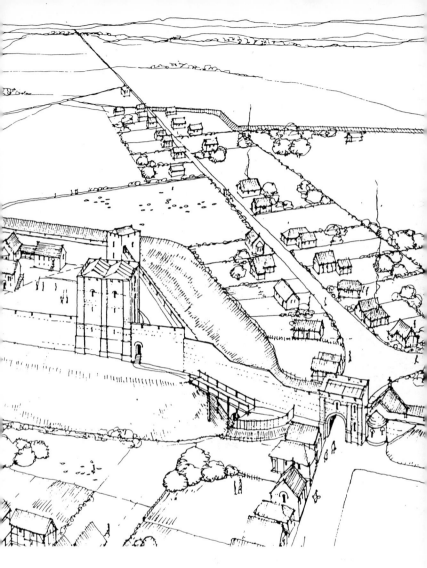

The castle was garrisoned by Royalist troops during the Civil War until its capture by Oliver Cromwell in 1645. A few years later, by order of Parliament, much of it was demolished, though the **Great Hall** was spared and still stands. This famous building is contemporary with Salisbury Cathedral and was built for Henry III by the same 'architect', Elias de Dereham. It is regarded by experts as second only to the medieval hall at Westminster. Until 1974, when new law courts nearby were opened, it was used for all Assize hearings and Quarter Sessions held in Winchester.

The east end of the Great Hall is covered with the names of knights of the shire (later termed County Members of Parliament) who represented Hampshire from the beginnings of the English system of representation in the 13th century until the Reform Acts of the last century. Here are repeated the names of men from prominent Hampshire families, men who no doubt looked after the interests of their county as if they were their own (which in many cases they were) — the Wallops, the Nortons, the Heathcotes and many others.

Winchester is a city from which much of the mystery of the past is being stripped by the careful researches of a new generation of scholars: undoubtedly the last 10–20 years will be seen as a 'golden age' of historical discovery in Hampshire. But one great question remains, namely: Who was King Arthur and where was his castle? Most scholars have given up believing in the existence of 'Arthur' and the tradition that Winchester was his Camelot. But the legend is so firmly placed that there might just be something in it.

One thing, however, is certain: the 'Round Table' that hangs at the west end of the Great Hall is a medieval fake.

INFORMATION

TOTTON TO ROMSEY   6 miles

How to get there: From Southampton take the A336 towards Cadnam and Salisbury. In Totton town centre reach start of walk along Test Wood Lane, the Test Way begins at the Salmon Leap Public House by Sterling Crescent. Free car parking by Library in town centre, ¼ mile walk to the Pub.

Public Transport: British Rail railway station at Totton, services from Southampton. Bus services from Southampton to Totton, Hampshire Bus 31, 32 and 33.

Where to park: Free car parking by Totton Library. ¼ mile walk to start of Test Way. Very limited verge car parking only near the Salmon Leap Pub.
Limited verge car parking near Nursling Manor Farm.

Where to stay: No accommodation in Totton but wide variety of Tourist Accommodation, hotels, guest houses and bed-and-breakfast, in Southampton. For free list contact Southampton Information Centre, Above Bar. Telephone 0703 221106.

Where to eat: Cafes and Pubs in Totton. Bakers for take-away food. Public House, The Salmon Leap, convenient for thirsty walkers.

TEST WAY ROUTE: From the Salmon Leap pub the path crosses the Test and then winds across marshland for a mile before crossing the river again and running alongside a railway line to a T-junction of minor roads. Here it turns left for a short distance and then right along a footpath opposite Manor Farm, before making a U-shaped detour under the M27 to Nursling, where it turns left. Just beyond the Parish Church it turns right alongside the river almost to Lea Park Farm, where it turns left and winds back to Moorcourt Farm. The path passes through the farmyard and turns right just before a bridge across the Blackwater tributary. It continues beside wooded river terraces until it reached the A31 Romsey–Cadnam road, where it turns right along the road for a few hundred yards and then left along the west bank of the river to Saddler's Mill and Romsey.

ROMSEY TO STOCKBRIDGE   11 miles

How to get there from Southampton: Take M271 to Nursling then A3057.

Public Transport: British Rail station at Romsey, services from Southampton via Eastleigh and on to Salisbury.
Bus services to Romsey:
from Southampton, Hampshire Bus 61, 62, 63, 63A
from Winchester, Hampshire Bus 66
from Salisbury, Hampshire Bus 34
For information telephone Winchester 53868.
Bus services to Stockbridge, Houghton, Horsebridge and King's Somborne, Hampshire Bus 91 from Winchester.

Where to park: Several car parks in Romsey (not free). Car park at Brook at southern end of restored railway line off A3057 Romsey to Stockbridge Road. Free car parking Stockbridge High Street.

Where to stay: Free accommodation list for Romsey and Test Valley from TIC Town Hall Car Park, Bridge Street, Andover. Telephone 0264 24320.

DAY-TO-DAY INFORMATION

Hotels and Inns in Romsey include:
Abbey Hotel, Dolphin Hotel, Sun Inn, Whitehorse Hotel.
Guest Houses and Bed and Breakfast in Romsey:
Mrs Dupont (Pauncefoot House) Romsey 0794 513139
Mrs Lamb, Romsey 514196
Mrs S Mason, Romsey 516557
Mrs N Dobson, Romsey 514909
Mrs P Edwards, Wessex Guest House, Romsey 512038
Mrs P Meredith, Romsey 512322
Mr & Mrs M Low, Romsey 515521
Miss Chambers, Romsey 512049.

Guest Houses and Bed and Breakfast in Sherfield English:
Mrs J Hayter, 07948 223
Mrs V Older, 07948 346

Guest Houses and Bed and Breakfast in Shootash and Mottisfont:
Mrs M Payne, 0794 22939
Mrs B Harris, 0794 513342
Mrs Mansbridge, 0794 515115
Mrs H Hall, 0794 68609
Mrs V Ayers (The Post Office), Lockerley 40243
Mrs Rolfe, 0794 40620.

Guest Houses and Bed and Breakfast in Houghton:
Mrs J R Shea, 0794 388551

Guest Houses and Bed and Breakfast in King's Somborne:
Mrs A T Brooke Webb, 0794 388420

Farmhouse Accommodation·
Mrs P Hillier, Butlers Wood Farm, Awbridge 0794 40368

Campsite:
Doctors Hill Farm, Sherfield English 0794 40402

Where to eat: Pubs, Cafes, etc. in Romsey. Bakers for take-away food. Pub, Dukes Head, near Timsbury. Post Office Cafe, Mottisfont. Pubs at Horsebridge and Houghton. Cafes and Pubs at Stockbridge.

Places to visit: Mottisfont Abbey and Gardens, National Trust.
Broadlands House, Romsey.
King John's House, Romsey.

TEST WAY ROUTE: About one and a half hours should be allowed for exploring Romsey and its Abbey. To return to the Test Way, take a footpath running west just to the south of Saddler's Mill and almost immediately take a right fork signposted to Squabb Wood. The path requires careful navigation in the centre of the wood (map reference SU335221): it enters a small clearing with an evergreen plantation along its left-hand side. A well-marked track goes up to the left but the Test Way continues a short way into the clearing before turning sharp right. It follows a narrow well-trodden path through woodland, past a huge dead beech tree on the right. It continues up to the left, then turns right and about a hundred yards ahead reaches a three-way sign: the Test Way turns right to a stile and a small stream. The way now cuts up across a field to the left and continues over a stile through sparse woodland to reach a minor road running west from Roke

Manor Farm. Turning left along the road and then, after a short distance, right along a footpath takes the route into a marked square-shaped depression. A farm track halfway along the right-hand edge of the square leads to the B3084 and Coles Farm Cottage opposite. The path continues along the left-hand side of the cottage, skirts round the east side of Awbridge and continues to Kimbridge Junction. A left turn just before the railway line soon takes the path over the line, and the River Dun, to Mottisfont church at a minor road. Turn left at the road and then right after a short distance, passing Mottisfont Abbey. A quarter of a mile beyond the Abbey the path turns right and runs across the valley of the Test towards Lower Brook. Hereafter it turns left and follows the route of the former railway line all the way to Stockbridge.

STOCKBRIDGE TO WHERWELL   5 miles

How to get there: From Winchester A272 Salisbury road.
From Southampton follow M217 and A3057 to Romsey then A3057 to Stockbridge via King's Somborne.

Public Transport: To Stockbridge from Winchester and Salisbury, Wilts & Dorset Bus X6. N.B. Thursday and Saturday only.
Hampshire Bus 91.
To Stockbridge from Andover, Hampshire Bus 277.
To Stockbridge from Salisbury, Hampshire Bus 277.
To Wherwell from Andover and Winchester, Hampshire Bus 99.
For information telephone Winchester 0962 52352.

Where to park: Free car parking at Stockbridge and West Down, Chilbolton. Limited verge car parking in Wherwell.

Where to stay: Free accommodation list from Andover TIC address above.
Hotels and Inns in Stockbridge:
Grosvenor Hotel
The Old Three Cups
The White Hart Inn
The White Lion, Wherwell.

Guest Houses and Bed and Breakfast:
Carberry Guest House, Stockbridge
Mr & Mrs Hooper, 0264 810771
Ms S Milligan, 0264 810866

Where to eat: Cafes and Pubs in Stockbridge. Bakery for take-away food. Pubs at Longstock (The Peat Spade) and Testcombe (The Mayfly). Pubs at Chilbolton and Wherwell. Village Shop at Wherwell.

TEST WAY ROUTE: At the east end of Stockbridge the Test Way follows the A30 and then the A3057 for several hundred yards before rejoining the old railway route, which it follows to Testcombe Bridge and the Mayfly pub, three and a half miles away. Here it passes under the road, turns right alongside a high wall and then crosses the Chilbolton road to West Down, an HCC open space. Once over the Down the Test Way returns briefly to the Chilbolton road, where it turns left along the road before turning right, alongside a branch of the river. It continues across the Memorial Playing Field and Chilbolton Common, crosses the two arms of the Test and then turns left along the Wherwell road for 50 yards before turning right to Wherwell village.

WHERWELL TO HURSTBOURNE TARRANT   15½ miles

How to get there: From Winchester. Take Andover road and B3420 to Wherwell. To St Mary Bourne and Hurstbourne take A34 to Whitchurch and B3084.

Public transport: From Winchester to Wherwell and Longparish, Hampshire Bus 99 (to Andover).
From Andover to Wherwell and Longparish, Hampshire Bus 99.
From Andover to St Mary Bourne and Hurstbourne Tarrant, Hampshire Bus 281.
From Newbury to Hurstbourne and St Mary Bourne, Hampshire Bus 281.

Where to park: Limited car parking in villages, otherwise vergeside car parking. Car park in St Mary Bourne.

Where to stay: Inn with accommodation, The White Lion, Wherwell.
Variety of Hotels in Andover, including:
Amberley Hotel, Bere Hill House Hotel, Danebury Hotel, White Hart Hotel.
Essebourne Manor Hotel, Hurstbourne Tarrant.
Bourne Valley Inn, St Mary Bourne.
The White Hart, Stoke.
Hurstbourne Inn, Hurstbourne Priors.

Guest Houses and Bed and Breakfast:
Mullion House, Andover, 0264 3520
Crossways House Guest House, Andover 0264 61055
Mrs E Ford, Andover, 0264 58121
Mrs J Walsh, Hurstbourne Tarrant, 0264 76229

Caravan & Camping Site:
Picket Piece, Andover, 0264 52048.

TEST WAY ROUTE: The path passes through Wherwell on the west side of its main street and then turns left towards New Barn, where it turns right and passes through Harewood Forest to the B3048 road to Longparish, a quarter of a mile south of the main A303 road. It crosses the B3048 to the hamlet of Gavelacre and then turns left to cross the A303 and continues by road to Longparish via Forton and Middleton. Beyond Longparish the path turns left just before the Plough Inn, passes through a recreation field and then turns right along Gladstone Terrace to meet a side road (alternatively: turn left into the side road after the Plough Inn), where it turns left and continues for one and a half miles to the B3400 by Fox Cottages. It passes briefly into the garden of a private house and then turns immediately to the right and continues anti-clockwise around the edge of a field to a gap in the hedge at the bottom. Hereafter it proceeds via track and road via Faulkners Down Farm to Lower Wyke Farm, where it turns right and runs to St Mary Bourne. It continues through the village to the George Inn in the summerhaugh (square) where it turns left across the Bourne Rivulet and into the recreation fields. The path now turns right, crosses a road to Upper Wyke Farm and then takes a route to Hurstbourne Tarrant via Swampton, where it strikes up to Stokehill Farm. There is a right of way through the grounds of the house, though the owners have also marked a suitable diversion. After passing through the copses of Wallop Hill Down, the way leads down to Hurstbourne Tarrant, meeting the road from St Mary Bourne opposite the church.

HURSTBOURNE TARRANT TO INKPEN   10 miles

How to get there: From Winchester take Andover road and A34 to Whitchurch then B3048 to St Mary Bourne and Hurstbourne Tarrant.
From Newbury to Hurstbourne Tarrant, Hampshire Bus 281.
From Andover to Inkpen Holt, Parnhams 282.
Andover 790382.
Crux Easton 283 Parnhams to Andover (school day).
From Newbury to Inkpen, Alder Valley 113, Alder Valley 0635 40743.
From Hungerford to Inkpen, Swansdown Coaches:
Information Inkpen 04884 234.

Where to park: Limited car parking at Hurstbourne Tarrant in village – free car park.

Where to stay: Hotel – Essebourne Manor, Hurstbourne Tarrant.
The Crown Inn, Upton.
Guest House – Mrs J Walsh, Durley Hill House, Hurstbourne Tarrant 0264 76229.
Hotels Hungerford:
The Bar Hotel
The Three Swans Hotel
Bed and Breakfast, Kintbury:
The Dundas Arms
Mr & Mrs Barr, 0488 58551
Mr & Mrs Warner, 0488 58256
For free accommodation list for Hungerford, Kintbury and Newbury contact Tourist Information Office, The Crossways, Newbury Telephone 0635 30267.

Where to eat: Village shop for picnic food, Hurstbourne Tarrant. The George & Dragon, Hurstbourne Tarrant, The Crown Inn, Upton, The Swan, Inkpen.

TEST WAY ROUTE: The Test Way passes through the village of Hurstbourne Tarrant via a path alongside Parsonage Farm, which lies alongside the parish church. It crosses the A343 Newbury–Andover road and runs along the side of the Bourne Rivulet to Ibthorpe. It passes in front of Ibthorpe Manor Farm and after a hundred yards turns right on a drove road that leads after three miles to the Upton–Linkenholt road, west of Rymers Barn. It turns right onto the road and then left after half a mile, at a crossroads beside a stable block with a clock tower. The path continues through Linkenholt past the church and in front of the Manor House, where it turns sharp right and after a hundred yards enters a field. It crosses the field, plunges down a little wooded gully and meets a 'yellow brick' road. It turns left along this track, keeping to the bottom of the valley, and after a mile, where the valley opens out and the woodland comes to an end, turns sharp right alongside woodland and continues across the steep slope of Sheepless Hill to Inkpen Hill.

THE CLARENDON WAY

SALISBURY   3 miles

How to get there: From Southampton. Follow M271 from Redbridge to Nursling M27(3), M27 to Cadnam and Ringwood, A36 from Junction 2 to Salisbury.
From Winchester take A30 to Stockbridge and Salisbury.
From Newbury take A343 to Salisbury via Hurstbourne Tarrant, Andover and Middle Wallop.

DAY-TO-DAY INFORMATION

Public transport: British Rail Station, services from Southampton via Eastleigh to Salisbury. From Winchester via Eastleigh. Bus Service to Salisbury from Newbury, Hampshire Bus 280 via Middle Wallop.
Bus Service to Salisbury from Winchester, Wilts & Dorset X6.
Bus Service to Salisbury from Southampton, Hampshire Bus 34.
Bus Information: Salisbury 0722 336855.

Where to park: Large car parks in centre of Salisbury.

Where to stay: Free accommodation list with many hotels, guest houses and bed and breakfast homes available from the Tourist Office, Fish Row, Salisbury 334956 334956.

Where to eat: Large variety of restaurants, pubs, cafes, bakeries and take-away food shops.

Places to visit: Mompeson House, National Trust.
Salisbury Cathedral.
Salisbury and South Wiltshire Museum.
Old Sarum.

CLARENDON WAY ROUTE: From Salisbury Cathedral Close take the High Street Gate and after a hundred yards turn right in New Canal, leading to Milford Street and Shady Bower. After a few hundred yards the road turns left into Manor Farm Road and then right along Milford Road to Milford Bridge. After a short distance the Clarendon Way takes a left-hand fork up Queen Manor Road and after a mile passes through a farmyard to run under a scarp slope to the right. About 500 yards further on a footpath strikes across a field and up the slope to emerge opposite King Manor Cottage. The path continues along the right-hand side of the cottage, with a conifer plantation on the right. On the left in the woodland are the remains of Clarendon Palace.

CLARENDON PALACE TO BROUGHTON   8 miles

How to get there: To Pitton from Salisbury take A30 out of Salisbury and take first turn to right after Pine Crest.
To Broughton from Winchester take A30 out of city and beyond Stockbridge take first turn left.

Public transport: Buses to Pitton and Winchester from Salisbury 48. Bells Coaches of Winterslow, information Winterslow 0980 862322.
Bus Service from Salisbury to Broughton, Hampshire Bus 277.
Bus Service from Winchester to Lopcombe Corner, near Middle Winterslow, Hampshire Bus 91.

Where to park: Very limited car parking in villages or on verges.

Where to stay: The Mount Motel, Stockbridge Road, Lopcombe.
The Pheasant Hotel, Winterslow.

Where to eat: Public Houses:
The Silver Plough, Pitton
The Lord Nelson, Middle Winterslow
The Lions Head, West Winterslow
The Greyhound Hotel, Broughton
Village shops in Pitton and Winterslow.

CLARENDON WAY ROUTE: The path continues along the track beside Clarendon Palace for a few hundred yards and then forks left into woodland, which it keeps to for two miles. It breaks out of the trees opposite Four Cottages, Pitton, and then continues behind the houses, past a school to a road. The way turns right along the road, passes over a bridge (and a dry river bed), after which it turns left at a crossroads and passes the parish church. Half-a-mile beyond the church the path turns right up a track and a steep scarp slope. At the top it takes a bridle path to All Saints Church, Winterslow. The path continues along the right-hand side of the churchyard, over a stile to a fork, where it takes the right-hand branch to meet the road at Middle Winterslow. It turns right along the road and through the village for a mile and then forks left along a road called The Causeway, which runs into a small recreation field. From here the path strikes up to the left under power cables to Red Lane, leading to The Shripple and Easton Common Hill. Here the Clarendon Way runs along the route of the former Roman road towards Upper Noads Copse and the county border. A mile further on at Buckholt Farm the path bears off to the left to Broughton, emerging alongside the Greyhound Pub opposite the parish church.

BROUGHTON TO OLIVER'S BATTERY   9½ miles

How to get there: To Broughton from Winchester take A30 to Stockbridge and continue out of village up hill. Take first turn on left.

Public transport: Bus service to Broughton from Salisbury, Hampshire Bus 277. Bus services to Broughton from Winchester, Hampshire Bus 91 to Stockbridge and Hampshire Bus 277 to Broughton.
Bus service to King's Somborne and Houghton from Winchester, Hampshire Bus 91.
Bus services between Oliver's Battery and Winchester City Centre, Hampshire Bus X66, 24, 25, 66.

Where to park: Limited free car parking in Broughton, Houghton and King's Somborne.
Free car parking at Horsebridge south of route (access along Test Way).
Free car parking at Farley Mount Country Park,

Where to stay: Bed and Breakfast accommodation:
Mr & Mrs J R Shea, Rowans Houghton 0794 388551
Mrs Brooke Webb, King's Somborne 0794 388420
The Old Market House, Broughton 0794 301249
See above for accommodation in Stockbridge.
Free accommodation list from Tourist Information, Town Mill Car Park, Bridge Street, Andover 0264 24320.
For free accommodation list contact Winchester Tourist Information Centre, The Broadway, Winchester 0962 68166.

Where to eat: Public Houses:
The Greyhound Hotel, Broughton
The Boot, Houghton
The Crown, King's Somborne
The Stanmore Hotel, Oliver's Battery.

CLARENDON WAY ROUTE: The Clarendon Way passes along the northern side of Broughton Church, across the Wallop Brook and then turns right to meet the Houghton–Mottisfont road after two miles. At this point it turns left along the road and then after a few hundred yards turns right to cross the River Test at a foot-bridge. On the east side of the valley the path crosses the Test Way, which the walker may wish to join. The Clarendon Way, however, climbs towards How Park Farm and then proceeds to King's Somborne Church, which can be seen from the top of the valley. Here it turns left along the road in front of the church (with the Crown Pub behind) and after a short distance left again at a T-junction. After a quarter of a mile a footpath turns right and a mile further on, near Hoplands, re-joins the route of the former Roman road, which it follows for a short distance. Then it turns to the south-east and continues along an old track lined with yew trees into a field. It crosses to the bottom of the field and turns left along a well-marked track to meet once more the line of the Roman road. At this point it turns half-right and takes a bridleway to the top of Beacon Hill. The way follows the ridge to Farley Mount Monument and then runs east alongside the old road for a mile, to a crossroads. The route continues ahead uphill past Crabwood House and then turns left into a no through road opposite the post box. The lane continues into an unmade track straight ahead. The track later is metalled and emerges at a crossroads. The Clarendon Way follows Kilham Lane as far as the roundabout at Romsey Road. Across the main road is Stanmore Lane and the route turns right in-to Olivers Battery Road North.

WINCHESTER   3 ½ miles

How to get there: From Salisbury, follow A30 through Stockbridge. From Southampton follow M271 and M27 to join A33 to Shawford, enter Winchester via St Cross.
From London M3 follow signs to Winchester.
From Portsmouth M27 and A33 (Trunk) to Winchester.

Public transport: British Rail station services from London Waterloo, Southampton and Portsmouth. Rail connection to Salisbury via Basingstoke.
Bus services from Southampton, Hampshire Bus X34 and 66. Bus services from Salisbury, Hampshire Bus X6 and Hampshire Bus 66 to Romsey then Hampshire Bus 24.
Bus services from Newbury, Hampshire Bus X34.
Bus services between City Centre to St Cross, Hampshire Bus X12, X34, 44, 47, 48, X65, 69, 69A, X69 and Alder Valley 214.

Where to park: Limited side street parking at St Cross.
Numerous car parks in Winchester City Centre.

Where to stay: For accommodation and visitors guide contact Winchester Tourist Information Centre, Winchester 0962 68166 (Price: postage).

Where to eat: Public Houses:
The Stanmore, Oliver's Battery
The Ben, St Cross
Bakery, St Cross
Numerous pubs, cafes, restaurants and take-away food shops in Winchester.

Places to visit: St Cross Hospital
Winchester College
Wolvesey Castle
Winchester Cathedral
The Great Hall

CLARENDON WAY ROUTE Clarendon Way continues across Badgers Farm Road into Olivers Battery Road South. At the shops the way turns left into Compton Way and left into Austin Close to the school gates. Then footpath to left around school site. Route crosses footbridge over main road and bears right onto track, then bears left down hill (White Shute Lane) to the railway line. Clarendon Way crosses the railway on footbridge and continues downhill on Mead Road to main road. Route continues along lane beside the Bell Public House to St Cross Hospital. Beyond the Hospital the way passes the City Centre past the Pumping Station in Garnier Road and Winchester College playing fields.

FURTHER READING

Aldrich, B   *The Ever-Rolling Stream*, 1984

Berrow, P,
Burbridge, B and
Genge, P   *The Story of Romsey*, 1984

Beddington, W G
and Christy E B
(eds)   *It Happened in Hampshire*, 4ed., 1966

Brode, A   *The Hampshire Village Book*, 1980

Bussby, F   *William Walker*, Winchester Cathedral, 1970 &
                           1983

Chandler, J   Endless Street: *A History of Salisbury and its
                           People*, 1983

Carpenter Turner, B *A History of Hampshire*, 1968

Carpenter Turner, B *Winchester*, 1980

Cobbett, W   *Rural Rides*, 1830

Cochran, C   *The Lost Roads of Wessex*, 1968

Cunliffe, B   *Danebury: Anatomy of an Iron Age Hillfort*,
                           1983

Dewar, G A B   *Wildlife in the Hampshire Highlands*, 1899

Edwards, A-M   *In the Steps of Jane Austen*, 2ed., 1985

Goodridge, E   *A History of the Hurstbourne and Fullerton
                           Railway*, 1984

FURTHER READING

Greene, H P — *Where the Bright Waters Meet*, 1924

Hadfield, C — *The Canals of South and South-East England*, 1969

Hawker, P — *Colonel Hawker's Shooting Diaries*, edited by E. Parker, 1931

Innes, K — *Life in a Hampshire Village*, 1944

Glenn, D F — *Rail Routes in Hampshire and East Dorset*, 1983

Hill, R — *A History of Stockbridge*, 1976

Hills, J W — *River Keeper*, 1934

— — *A Summer on The Test*, 1946

Knowles, C — *Sparsholt and Lainston*, with a chapter by D E Johnston on Sparsholt Roman Villa, 1981

Lockyer, E M — *Chilbolton Fragments: Story of a Test Valley Village*, 1984

Mace, P B — *It Won't Last for Ever But It's Not Done For Yet*, Winchester Cathedral, 1973

Merritt, A L — *A Hamlet in Old Hampshire*, 1902

Moore, P (ed) — *A Guide to the Industrial Archaeology of Hampshire and The Isle of Wight*, 1984

Moutray Read, D H — *Highways and Byways in Hampshire*, 1908

O'Dell, N — *The River Test*, 1979

Patterson, A. Temple, — *Southampton: A Biography*, 1970

Pevsner, N B L and Lloyd D — *Buildings of England: Hampshire and Isle of Wight*, 1967

Pevsner, N B L and B Cherry — *Buildings of England: Wiltshire*, 1975

Sabben-Clare, J — *Winchester College*, 1981

Shennan, S J and
Schadla Hall, R T
(eds)   *The Archaeology of Hampshire*, 1981

Shurlock, Barry   *Portrait of the Solent*, 1983

Snagge, G   *Letters from Longstock*, 1968

—   *More Letters from Longstock*, 1971

Stevens, J   *A Parochial History of St Mary Bourne*, 1888

Street, P   *Portrait of Wiltshire*, 1971

Varley, T   *Hampshire*, 1909

Vesey-Fitzgerald, B   *Hampshire and the Isle of Wight*, 1949

—   *The Hampshire Avon*, 1950

—   *Winchester*, 1953

Whitlock, R   *A Family and a Village*, 1969

Woodland, W L   *The Story of Winchester*, 1932

Woodruffe, B J   *Wiltshire Villages*, 1982

INDEX TO PLACES

Illustrations

Dean and Chapter of Winchester Cathedral: 110.

Hampshire Field Club: 59.

Hampshire Recreation: 36/37, 41.

Hampshire Libraries: 47.

A. Harvey: 21, 28/29, 32, 34, 53, 57, 64.

J. Holder: 13, 23, 39.

E. Lane: 105, 109, 112/113.

D. Moldon: 10/11, 14/15, 25, 77, 85, 89, 93, 97, 101.

Drive Publications: 73.

J. Reynolds: 114/115.

Salisbury District Council: 68/69.

Salisbury Museum: 81.

B. Shurlock: 45, 63.

Hampshire County Council Planning Dept.: 59.

The illustration on page 73 is taken from AA Book of
Country Walks, Drive Publications, London. Copyright
© 1975. Used with permission.